Ninja MC1101 Foodi Possible Cooker Pro Cookbook for Beginners

2000 Days of Easy 8-in-1 Soups & Stews Recipes for One-Pot Cooking, Including Slow Cook, Sear/Sauté, Braise, and More!

Iderling Qawthory

Table of Contents

INTRODUCTION

Structural Composition of the Ninja MC1101

The Ninja MC1101, with its 8-in-1 versatility, serves as a multifunctional kitchen appliance designed to streamline your cooking experience. Let's delve into the structural composition of this innovative cooker to understand how it combines various functionalities seamlessly.

- Base Unit:

    The foundation of the Ninja MC1101 is the base unit, housing the electrical components and the control panel. This unit serves as the brain of the appliance, allowing users to choose from a range of cooking options with adjustable temperature control. The cool-touch side handles ensure safe transport when needed.

- 6.5-qt Cooking Pot:

    The heart of the Ninja MC1101 is the 6.5-quart cooking pot, crafted with durability in mind. The pot accommodates family-sized meals, making it perfect for weekly meal prepping or gatherings. Its cast stainless steel handles offer a secure grip, allowing for easy handling even when hot.

- Oven-Safe Glass Lid:

    The appliance features an oven-safe glass lid that can withstand

temperatures up to 500°F. This lid is essential for the cooker-to-oven transition, enabling users to achieve a crispy finish on their dishes. The transparency of the glass lid allows for convenient monitoring of the cooking process without lifting the lid and releasing heat.

- Rice Spoon:

Included in the package is a specialized rice spoon designed for easy scooping and serving. This utensil complements the cooker's versatility, especially when preparing rice dishes. The design ensures gentle handling of cooked grains, preventing them from becoming mushy.

- Versatile Cooking Functions:

The Ninja MC1101 is engineered to replace 10 different kitchen tools, consolidating the clutter on countertops. Its 8-in-1 versatility covers slow

cooking, searing/sautéing, braising, keeping warm, and specific settings for white rice, brown rice, oats, and pasta. This diversity allows users to experiment with a wide range of recipes, from savory stews to perfectly cooked grains.

- One-Pot Cooking Efficiency:

The design promotes easy, one-pot cooking, enabling users to prepare mains and grains together or separately within the same compact system. The efficiency of this approach is underscored by the cooker's ability to operate 30% faster than traditional cooking methods, facilitating quicker meal preparation.

- Family-Sized Capacity:

With a generous 6.5-quart capacity, the Ninja MC1101 caters to the needs

of larger households. It can accommodate four 6-ounce chicken breasts or a substantial 7-pound roast, making it an ideal choice for those who prioritize batch cooking or entertaining guests.

- Faster Rice Cooking:

The Ninja MC1101 stands out in its ability to cook rice 50% faster than traditional rice cookers. This feature is particularly advantageous for busy individuals or families who seek efficient meal solutions without compromising on the quality of their rice dishes.

- Cooker to Oven to Table Convenience:

The cooker's versatility extends to its seamless transition from cooker to oven, allowing users to finish their dishes in the oven for added texture or browning. The ability to serve directly from the pot simplifies the dining

experience, minimizing the need for additional serving dishes.

- Dishwasher-Safe Components:

  Cleaning up after cooking is a breeze, as the 6.5-qt cooking pot, lid, and rice spoon are all dishwasher safe. This feature enhances the overall convenience of the Ninja MC1101, ensuring that maintaining the appliance is as straightforward as using it.

In summary, the structural composition of the Ninja MC1101 reflects a thoughtful integration of components aimed at providing users with a versatile, efficient, and user-friendly cooking experience. From the durable cooking pot to the oven-safe lid and the array of cooking functions, this kitchen appliance stands as a testament to innovation in modern culinary technology.

Function of This Appliance

The Ninja Cooker boasts an impressive 8-in-1 versatility, functioning as a slow cooker, sear/sauté pan, braiser, food warmer, and rice cooker, as well as being able to handle white rice, brown rice, oats, and pasta. This multifunctional appliance is designed to streamline your kitchen by replacing the need for 10 different tools, including a slow cooker, nonstick pot, sauté pan, cast iron skillet, and more.

One of the standout features of this appliance is its ability to facilitate easy, one-pot cooking. With the Ninja Cooker, you can prepare both main courses and grains together or cook them separately in a single compact cooking system. This not only saves time but also offers a 30% faster cooking process compared to traditional methods. This efficiency is particularly beneficial for busy individuals or families seeking to minimize cooking time without compromising on the quality of their meals.

The family-sized capacity of 6.5 quarts makes the Ninja Cooker ideal for weekly meal prepping and preparing large, family-sized meals. The spacious pot can accommodate four 6-ounce chicken breasts or a 7-pound roast, providing enough food to serve up to six people. This makes it a practical choice for gatherings, family dinners, or batch cooking for the week.

Moreover, the Ninja Cooker takes speed to the next level by allowing you to cook rice 50% faster than with a traditional rice cooker. This feature is a game-changer for those who frequently incorporate rice into their meals but want to expedite the cooking process.

The versatility of this appliance extends beyond its primary functions, as the oven-safe pot can withstand temperatures up to 500°F. This enables users to seamlessly transfer the pot from the cooker to the oven for a crispy finish on dishes. The included rice spoon makes serving easy, allowing you to present your creations directly from the pot to the table.

The compact design of the Ninja Cooker ensures a small countertop footprint, making it suitable for everyday use in kitchens with limited space. Its sleek and efficient design aligns with the contemporary demand for appliances that blend functionality with aesthetics.

The adjustable temperature control feature adds another layer of control to your cooking experience. Whether you're aiming for a perfect sear or prefer low and slow cooking to tenderize meats, the Ninja Cooker allows you to customize the cooking process to suit your preferences.

In terms of maintenance, the Ninja Cooker prioritizes convenience. The pot, lid, and rice spoon are all dishwasher safe, simplifying the cleaning process and ensuring that the appliance remains ready for the next culinary adventure.

In conclusion, the Ninja Cooker is a versatile and efficient kitchen appliance designed to simplify and enhance the cooking experience. From its 8-in-1 functionality to its family-sized capacity and time-saving features, this appliance caters to a wide range of cooking needs. Its ability to replace multiple kitchen tools and facilitate easy one-pot cooking makes it a valuable addition to any kitchen, providing both convenience and culinary creativity to its users.

Tips and Tricks to Using Your Cooker

Unlocking the full potential of your Ninja MC1101 Foodi Everyday Possible Cooker can revolutionize your kitchen experience. Here are some tips and tricks to make the most out of its 8-in-1 versatility:

- Mastering Slow Cooking:

    Utilize the slow cook function for tender and flavorful dishes. Plan ahead

for busy days by letting your meals simmer throughout the day.

Optimize the cooker's one-pot capability by combining ingredients for stews, soups, or roasts.

- Searing/Sautéing Excellence:

Achieve a perfect sear on meats before slow cooking to enhance flavors.

Sauté aromatic ingredients like onions and garlic directly in the cooker for added depth to your dishes.

- Braising Brilliance:

Master the art of braising by searing your protein, adding liquid, and slow cooking for succulent results.

Experiment with different braising liquids such as broth, wine, or sauces to create diverse flavor profiles.

- Efficient Keep Warm Feature:

Use the keep warm function to maintain the ideal serving temperature for your dishes, especially helpful when preparing multiple components for a meal.

Ensure optimal food safety by utilizing the keep warm feature when entertaining or serving buffet-style meals.

- Rice and Grain Cooking Mastery:

Take advantage of the cooker's ability to cook various types of rice and grains, saving time and kitchen space.

Experiment with different rice varieties and explore the perfect settings for achieving the desired texture.

- Oats and Pasta Perfection:

Prepare wholesome breakfasts with oats cooked to perfection in the Ninja Cooker.

Cook pasta directly in the pot for a one-pot pasta experience, reducing the need for additional cookware.

- Family-Sized Meal Prep:

Leverage the generous 6.5-qt capacity for efficient weekly meal prepping.

Batch cook family-sized meals and freeze portions for convenient, ready-to-eat options.

- Speedy Cooking Advantage:

Save time with the Ninja Cooker's 30% faster cooking compared to traditional methods.

Utilize the 50% faster rice cooking feature for quick and convenient side dishes.

- Seamless Cooker to Oven Transitions:

Take advantage of the oven-safe pot, allowing you to transfer dishes from the cooker to the oven for finishing touches like a crispy crust or browning.

Streamline your cooking process by minimizing the number of dishes used.

- Compact Countertop Convenience:

Appreciate the space-saving design of the Ninja Cooker, fitting easily into your everyday kitchen routine.

Keep your countertop clutter-free by replacing multiple kitchen tools with this all-in-one appliance.

- Adjustable Temperature Control Expertise:

Experiment with the adjustable temperature control to achieve the perfect sear or slow cook for tenderization.

Customize cooking temperatures for various recipes, unlocking a wide range of culinary possibilities.

- Effortless Cleaning with Dishwasher Safe Components:

Simplify cleanup by placing the pot, lid, and rice spoon in the dishwasher.

Ensure the longevity of your Ninja Cooker by maintaining regular cleaning practices.

Incorporating these tips and tricks into your cooking routine will transform your Ninja MC1101 Foodi Everyday Possible Cooker into a versatile and indispensable kitchen companion, providing efficiency, flavor, and convenience in every meal.

Explore More Recipe Inspiration In This Book

The Ninja Cooker is a versatile kitchen appliance that promises to simplify your cooking experience by replacing 10 different kitchen tools. With its 8-in-1 functionality, it offers a wide range of cooking options, making it a valuable addition to any kitchen. The included recipe book is a treasure trove of culinary inspiration, allowing you to unleash the full potential of your Ninja Cooker.

One of the standout features of the Ninja Cooker is its 8-in-1 versatility. From slow cooking to searing/sautéing, braising, and keeping warm, to preparing various types of rice, oats, and pasta, this appliance is designed to handle

a multitude of cooking tasks. The recipe book takes full advantage of these functions, providing you with recipes that showcase the diverse capabilities of the Ninja Cooker.

The book not only serves as a guide to making the most of your Ninja Cooker but also as a source of creative cooking ideas. It explores recipes that leverage the appliance's ability to cook mains and grains together or separately, promoting easy one-pot cooking. The convenience of preparing meals in one compact cooking system is highlighted, with the added benefit of being 30% faster than traditional cooking methods.

One of the key advantages of the Ninja Cooker is its family-sized capacity. With a 6.5-qt capacity, it's perfect for meal prepping and preparing family-sized meals. The recipe book includes dishes that cater to this capacity, allowing you to cook enough to feed up to six people. From four 6-oz chicken breasts to a 7-lb roast, the Ninja Cooker ensures you can prepare hearty meals for your loved ones with ease.

The faster cooking feature of the Ninja Cooker is not overlooked in the recipe book. With the ability to cook rice 50% faster than traditional rice cookers, the appliance adds efficiency to your kitchen routine. The book provides recipes that make the most of this time-saving capability, allowing you to enjoy delicious rice dishes in less time.

The cooker's versatility extends beyond the kitchen, as it is designed for seamless transitions from cooker to oven to table. The oven-safe pot, capable of withstanding temperatures up to 500°F, allows you to achieve a crispy finish by transferring the pot from the cooker to the oven. The recipe book guides you through this process, ensuring that your meals are not only cooked to perfection but also presented in style.

The compact design of the Ninja Cooker is emphasized in the book, highlighting its small countertop footprint. This makes it an ideal choice for everyday use, ensuring that it doesn't take up unnecessary space in your kitchen. The adjustable temperature control is explored in various recipes, allowing you to customize the cooking process for the perfect sear or a slow-cooked, tender result.

Cleaning up after cooking is often a daunting task, but the Ninja Cooker aims to simplify it. The dishwasher-safe pot, lid, and rice spoon ensure easy and convenient cleaning, saving you time and effort. The recipe book acknowledges the importance of hassle-free cleanup, encouraging you to enjoy your meals without the worry of a lengthy post-cooking cleanup process.

In conclusion, the recipe book for the Ninja Cooker is a valuable resource for anyone looking to explore the full potential of this versatile kitchen appliance. From quick and efficient cooking to family-sized meals and creative one-pot recipes, the book offers a diverse range of culinary inspiration. Whether you're a seasoned chef or a novice in the kitchen, the Ninja Cooker and its accompanying recipe book make the art of cooking enjoyable, efficient, and accessible.

Troubleshooting Guide

The Ninja Cooker is a versatile kitchen appliance that combines multiple functions to simplify your cooking experience. However, like any appliance, it may encounter issues from time to time. This troubleshooting guide is designed to help you identify and resolve common problems you might face with your Ninja Cooker.

Power Issues:

- Problem: The Ninja Cooker is not turning on.
- Solution: Ensure that the unit is properly plugged in and that the power source is functional. Check if the power outlet is working by plugging in another device. If the issue persists, contact Ninja customer support.

Display Problems:

- Problem: The digital display is not working or showing incorrect information.
- Solution: Check the power connection and try unplugging and plugging in the unit again. If the display still doesn't work, it might be a malfunction, and you should contact Ninja customer support for assistance.

Temperature Control Issues:

- Problem: The Ninja Cooker is not reaching the desired temperature.
- Solution: Ensure that you have selected the correct cooking mode and adjusted the temperature accordingly. If the problem persists, there might be an issue with the internal thermostat. Contact Ninja customer support for further guidance.

Cooking Time Discrepancies:

- Problem: The cooking times are inconsistent or longer than expected.
- Solution: Check if you are using the appropriate cooking mode for the recipe. Ensure that the ingredients are fresh and properly prepared. If the issue continues, consider recalibrating your cooking times based on your specific unit's performance.

Uneven Cooking:

- Problem: Food is cooking unevenly.
- Solution: Stir or rotate the ingredients during cooking to promote even heat distribution. Make sure the cooking pot is properly placed on the cooking base. If the problem persists, there may be an issue with the heating element, and you should contact Ninja customer support.

Steam Leakage:

- Problem: Steam is escaping from the Ninja Cooker during operation.
- Solution: Ensure that the lid is properly sealed and that the steam vent is not blocked. Check for any damages to the sealing gasket and replace it if necessary. If the issue persists, contact Ninja customer support.

Overheating:

- Problem: The Ninja Cooker is overheating.
- Solution: Turn off the unit immediately and unplug it. Allow it to cool down before attempting to use it again. Ensure that the cooking base is clean and free from any obstructions. If the problem persists, contact Ninja customer support.

Sticking or Burning Food:

- Problem: Food is sticking to the bottom of the pot or burning.
- Solution: Make sure to adequately grease the pot before cooking. Adjust the temperature and cooking time based on the recipe. If the issue continues, consider using a lower heat setting or adding more liquid to the recipe.

By following this troubleshooting guide, you can address common issues with your Ninja Cooker and enjoy its multifunctional capabilities with ease. If problems persist or are not covered in this guide, reaching out to Ninja customer support is recommended for professional assistance. Regular maintenance, proper usage, and adherence to the provided guidelines will contribute to the optimal performance of your Ninja Cooker.

Chapter 1: Breakfast

Spinach and Feta Pasta Scramble

Prep Time: 12 Minutes   Cook Time: 18 Minutes   Serves: 4

Ingredients:

- 8 oz rotini pasta
- 1 cup chopped fresh spinach
- 1/2 cup crumbled feta cheese
- 4 large eggs, beaten
- Salt and pepper to taste

Directions:

1. Cook rotini pasta using the "Pasta" function in the Ninja Foodi Cooker.
2. In a pan, combine cooked pasta, chopped spinach, and crumbled feta cheese.
3. Pour beaten eggs over the pasta mixture and stir continuously until eggs are scrambled and fully cooked.
4. Season with salt and pepper to taste.
5. Serve the pasta scramble warm for a savory and protein-packed breakfast!

Nutritional Value (Amount per Serving):

Calories: 182; Fat: 8.97; Carb: 18.54; Protein: 7.29

Mediterranean Pasta Salad with Sun-Dried Tomatoes

Prep Time: 15 Minutes   Cook Time: 12 Minutes   Serves: 4

Ingredients:

- 8 oz bowtie pasta
- 1/2 cup sliced black olives
- 1/2 cup crumbled feta cheese
- 1/4 cup chopped sun-dried tomatoes
- 2 tablespoons olive oil
- Fresh basil leaves for garnish

Directions:

1. Cook bowtie pasta using the "Pasta" function in the Ninja Foodi Cooker.
2. In a large bowl, combine cooked pasta, sliced black olives, crumbled feta cheese, and chopped sun-dried tomatoes.
3. Drizzle olive oil over the pasta salad and toss until well combined.
4. Garnish with fresh basil leaves before serving.
5. Enjoy a Mediterranean-inspired pasta salad for a light and flavorful breakfast.

Nutritional Value (Amount per Serving):

Calories: 189; Fat: 11.26; Carb: 18.48; Protein: 4.64

Cheesy Garlic Pasta

Prep Time: 20 Minutes   Cook Time: 30 Minutes   Serves: 4

Ingredients:

- 8 oz penne pasta
- 1 cup shredded mozzarella cheese
- 1/2 cup grated Parmesan cheese
- 1/4 cup chopped fresh parsley
- 2 cloves garlic, minced
- 1 can (14 oz) diced tomatoes, drained

Directions:

1. Cook penne pasta using the "Pasta" function in the Ninja Foodi Cooker.
2. In a dish, combine cooked pasta, mozzarella cheese, Parmesan cheese, chopped parsley, minced garlic, and diced tomatoes.
3. Mix well and cook in the Ninja Foodi Cooker using the "Braise" function at medium temperature for 15 minutes or until cheese is melted and bubbly.
4. Serve the cheesy garlic pasta hot.

Nutritional Value (Amount per Serving):

Calories: 175; Fat: 4.05; Carb: 20.93; Protein: 14.58

Shrimp and Asparagus Oat Risotto

Prep Time: 15 Minutes   Cook Time: 25 Minutes   Serves: 4

Ingredients:

- 1 cup steel-cut oats
- 4 cups chicken broth
- 1/2 lb shrimp, peeled and deveined
- 1 bunch asparagus, trimmed and chopped
- 1/4 cup grated Pecorino Romano cheese
- 2 tablespoons olive oil

Directions:

1. In the Ninja Foodi Cooker, combine steel-cut oats and chicken broth. Set the cooker to the "Oats" function for 15 minutes.
2. While oats are cooking, sauté shrimp and asparagus in olive oil until shrimp are cooked and asparagus is tender.
3. Stir cooked shrimp and asparagus into the oats.
4. Mix in grated Pecorino Romano cheese and serve the oat risotto hot.

Nutritional Value (Amount per Serving):

Calories: 591; Fat: 27.59; Carb: 20.48; Protein: 70.53

Maple Pecan Pasta Parfait

Prep Time: 10 Minutes   Cook Time: 20 Minutes   Serves: 4

Ingredients:

- 8 oz fettuccine pasta
- 1 cup chopped pecans
- 1/2 cup maple syrup
- 1/2 cup Greek yogurt
- 1 teaspoon vanilla extract

Directions:

1. Cook fettuccine pasta using the "Pasta" function in the Ninja Foodi Cooker.
2. In a pan, toast chopped pecans until fragrant.
3. Mix maple syrup and vanilla extract into the toasted pecans.
4. Layer cooked pasta, maple pecan mixture, and Greek yogurt in parfait glasses.
5. Repeat layers and finish with a drizzle of maple syrup. Enjoy a sweet and nutty pasta parfait for breakfast!

Nutritional Value (Amount per Serving):

Calories: 365; Fat: 18.36; Carb: 46.81; Protein: 6.67

Avocado Pesto Pasta

Prep Time: 15 Minutes   Cook Time: 20 Minutes   Serves: 4

Ingredients:

- 8 oz linguine pasta
- 2 ripe avocados
- 1 cup fresh basil leaves
- 1/2 cup grated Parmesan cheese
- 1/4 cup pine nuts
- Juice of 1 lemon
- Salt and pepper to taste

Directions:

1. Cook linguine pasta using the "Pasta" function in the Ninja Foodi Cooker.
2. In a blender, combine avocados, basil leaves, Parmesan cheese, pine nuts, lemon juice, salt, and pepper.
3. Blend until smooth, adjusting consistency with a bit of water if needed.
4. Toss the cooked pasta with the avocado pesto sauce.
5. Serve immediately.

Nutritional Value (Amount per Serving):

Calories: 349; Fat: 24.46; Carb: 29.14; Protein: 8.48

Chai Spiced Oatmeal

Prep Time: 8 Minutes   Cook Time: 15 Minutes   Serves: 4

Ingredients:

- 2 cups rolled oats
- 4 cups chai tea (brewed and cooled)
- 1/2 cup chopped nuts (almonds, walnuts)
- 1/4 cup raisins
- 2 tablespoons honey
- 1 teaspoon ground cinnamon

Directions:

1. In the Ninja Foodi Cooker, combine rolled oats and brewed chai tea. Set the cooker to the "Oats" function for 15 minutes.
2. Stir in chopped nuts, raisins, honey, and ground cinnamon.
3. Cook until the oats are creamy and the flavors are well combined.
4. Serve the chai spiced oatmeal hot.

Nutritional Value (Amount per Serving):

Calories: 255; Fat: 12.24; Carb: 44.17; Protein: 12.41

Tomato Basil Pasta Frittata

Prep Time: 15 Minutes   Cook Time: 25 Minutes   Serves: 4

Ingredients:

- 8 oz fusilli pasta
- 1 cup cherry tomatoes, halved
- 1/2 cup fresh basil leaves, chopped
- 1/2 cup grated Parmesan cheese
- 6 large eggs, beaten
- Salt and pepper to taste

Directions:

1. Cook fusilli pasta using the "Pasta" function in the Ninja Foodi Cooker.
2. In a bowl, mix cooked pasta, cherry tomatoes, chopped basil, and grated Parmesan cheese.
3. Pour beaten eggs over the pasta mixture and season with salt and pepper.
4. Set the cooker to the "Sear/Saute" function at medium temperature and cook until the frittata is set.
5. Slice and serve the tomato basil pasta frittata.

Nutritional Value (Amount per Serving):

Calories: 212; Fat: 10.69; Carb: 19.87; Protein: 9.34

Caprese Pasta Breakfast Bowl

Prep Time: 15 Minutes   Cook Time: 20 Minutes   Serves: 4

Ingredients:

- 8 oz penne pasta
- 1 cup cherry tomatoes, halved
- 1 cup fresh mozzarella balls
- 1/4 cup fresh basil leaves, torn
- 2 tablespoons balsamic glaze
- 4 poached eggs

Directions:

1. Cook penne pasta using the "Pasta" function in the Ninja Foodi Cooker.
2. In a bowl, combine cooked pasta, cherry tomatoes, fresh mozzarella balls, and torn basil leaves.
3. Drizzle with balsamic glaze and toss gently.
4. Poach eggs separately and place one on top of each pasta bowl.
5. Serve the Caprese pasta breakfast bowl warm.

Nutritional Value (Amount per Serving):

Calories: 227; Fat: 10.27; Carb: 22.9; Protein: 11.46

Peach Cobbler Oatmeal

Prep Time: 10 Minutes   Cook Time: 15 Minutes   Serves: 4

Ingredients:

- 2 cups rolled oats
- 4 cups milk (dairy or plant-based)
- 2 ripe peaches, diced
- 1/4 cup brown sugar
- 1 teaspoon ground cinnamon
- 1/2 cup granola for topping

Directions:

1. In the Ninja Foodi Cooker, combine rolled oats, milk, diced peaches, brown sugar, and ground cinnamon.
2. Set the cooker to the "Oats" function for 15 minutes.
3. Stir occasionally to ensure the oats are creamy and the peaches are softened.
4. Serve the peach cobbler oatmeal in bowls, topped with granola for added crunch.

Nutritional Value (Amount per Serving):

Calories: 436; Fat: 12.65; Carb: 85.13; Protein: 16.73

Pesto Veggie Pasta Scramble

Prep Time: 15 Minutes   Cook Time: 20 Minutes   Serves: 4

Ingredients:

- 8 oz rotini pasta
- 1/2 cup basil pesto
- 1 cup diced bell peppers (mixed colors)
- 1 cup zucchini, diced
- 1 cup cherry tomatoes, halved
- 4 large eggs, beaten
- Salt and pepper to taste

Directions:

1. Cook rotini pasta using the "Pasta" function in the Ninja Foodi Cooker.
2. In a pan, sauté diced bell peppers, zucchini, and cherry tomatoes until tender.
3. Stir in basil pesto and cooked pasta.
4. Pour beaten eggs over the pasta-vegetable mixture and cook until eggs are scrambled and fully cooked.
5. Season with salt and pepper to taste.
6. Serve the pesto veggie pasta scramble warm.

Nutritional Value (Amount per Serving):

Calories: 138; Fat: 5.01; Carb: 19.06; Protein: 4.83

Oats and Spinach Stuffed Mushrooms

Prep Time: 20 Minutes   Cook Time: 30 Minutes   Serves: 4

Ingredients:

- 8 large mushrooms, stems removed
- 1 cup old-fashioned oats
- 1 cup vegetable broth
- 1 cup fresh spinach, chopped
- 1/2 cup feta cheese, crumbled
- 2 tablespoons olive oil
- 1 teaspoon dried oregano
- Salt and pepper to taste

Directions:

1. Set the Ninja Foodi Cooker to "Oats" mode.
2. Place mushrooms in the pot, cap side down.
3. In a separate bowl, mix oats with vegetable broth. Add chopped spinach,

feta cheese, olive oil, oregano, salt, and pepper. Stir well.

4. Spoon the oat and spinach mixture into the mushrooms.
5. Cook the stuffed mushrooms until the filling is heated through and mushrooms are tender.
6. Transfer to a serving plate and enjoy these flavorful stuffed mushrooms.

Nutritional Value (Amount per Serving):

Calories: 187; Fat: 12.61; Carb: 20.09; Protein: 8.61

Air Fryer Greek Frittata

Prep Time: 8 Minutes   Cook Time: 10 Minutes   Serves: 4

Ingredients:

- 2 cups rolled oats
- 2 cups mixed berries (strawberries, blueberries, raspberries)
- 2 cups yogurt (dairy or plant-based)
- 1/4 cup honey or maple syrup
- Granola for topping

Directions:

1. In a blender, combine rolled oats, mixed berries, yogurt, and honey/maple syrup.
2. Set the cooker to the "Oats" function for 10 minutes.
3. Cook and blend until smooth, adding more liquid if needed.
4. Divide the smoothie into bowls and top with granola.
5. Serve immediately.

Nutritional Value (Amount per Serving):

Calories: 585; Fat: 23.85; Carb: 96.76; Protein: 15.52

Apple Cinnamon Overnight Oats

Prep Time: 5 Minutes   Cook Time: 10 Minutes   Serves: 4

Ingredients:

- 2 cups rolled oats
- 2 cups milk (dairy or plant-based)
- 1 large apple, diced
- 1/4 cup maple syrup
- 1 teaspoon ground cinnamon

Directions:

1. In a bowl, combine rolled oats, milk, diced apple, maple syrup, and ground cinnamon.
2. Set the cooker to the "Oats" function and cook for 10 minutes.

3. Divide the mixture into individual jars or containers and refrigerate overnight.
4. In the morning, give it a good stir and serve chilled.
5. Enjoy the delightful combination of apple and cinnamon for a comforting breakfast!

Nutritional Value (Amount per Serving):

Calories: 272; Fat: 7.41; Carb: 58.38; Protein: 12.15

Mediterranean Oat Salad

Prep Time: 10 Minutes   Cook Time: 10 Minutes   Serves: 4

Ingredients:

- 2 cups rolled oats
- 1 cup diced cucumber
- 1 cup cherry tomatoes, halved
- 1/2 cup Kalamata olives, sliced
- 1/2 cup crumbled feta cheese
- 1/4 cup olive oil
- Fresh oregano for garnish

Directions:

1. In a bowl, combine rolled oats, diced cucumber, cherry tomatoes, sliced olives, and crumbled feta cheese.
2. Set the cooker to the "Oats" function and cook for 10 minutes.
3. Drizzle olive oil over the salad and toss until well combined.
4. Garnish with fresh oregano before serving.

Nutritional Value (Amount per Serving):

Calories: 327; Fat: 22.94; Carb: 38.81; Protein: 11.77

Almond Joy Overnight Oats

Prep Time: 5 Minutes   Cook Time: 8 Minutes   Serves: 4

Ingredients:

- 2 cups rolled oats
- 2 cups almond milk
- 1/4 cup shredded coconut
- 1/4 cup chopped almonds
- 1/4 cup chocolate chips
- 2 tablespoons honey or maple syrup

Directions:

1. In a bowl, combine rolled oats, almond milk, shredded coconut, chopped almonds, chocolate chips, and honey/maple syrup.
2. Set the cooker to the "Oats" function and cook for 8 minutes.
3. Divide the mixture into individual jars or containers and refrigerate

overnight.

4. In the morning, stir well and enjoy the indulgent flavors of almond joy in your oatmeal!

Nutritional Value (Amount per Serving):

Calories: 275; Fat: 8.15; Carb: 59.3; Protein: 9.75

Peanut Butter Banana Overnight Oats

Prep Time: 5 Minutes   Cook Time: 10 Minutes   Serves: 4

Ingredients:

- 2 cups rolled oats
- 2 cups milk (dairy or plant-based)
- 1/2 cup peanut butter
- 2 ripe bananas, mashed
- 1/4 cup honey or maple syrup

Directions:

1. In a bowl, combine rolled oats, milk, peanut butter, mashed bananas, and honey/maple syrup.
2. Set the cooker to the "Oats" function and cook for 10 minutes.
3. Divide the mixture into individual jars or containers and refrigerate overnight.
4. In the morning, stir well and enjoy a delicious peanut butter and banana oatmeal!

Nutritional Value (Amount per Serving):

Calories: 401; Fat: 15.99; Carb: 69; Protein: 14.77

Chapter 2: Grains and Staples

Quinoa and Black Bean Power Bowl

Prep Time: 15 Minutes   Cook Time: 20 Minutes   Serves: 4

Ingredients:

- 1 cup quinoa, rinsed
- 2 cups vegetable broth
- 1 can (15 oz) black beans, drained and rinsed
- 1 cup corn kernels (fresh or frozen)
- 1 avocado, diced
- 1 lime, juiced
- 2 tablespoons olive oil
- Cilantro for garnish
- Salt and pepper to taste

Directions:

1. Rinse quinoa under cold water. In the Ninja Foodi Cooker, combine quinoa and vegetable broth. Select the 'White Rice' function and cook for 15 minutes.
2. In a separate bowl, mix black beans and corn. Set aside.
3. Once quinoa is cooked, fluff it with a fork. Combine with the black bean and corn mixture. Add diced avocado.
4. In a small bowl, whisk together lime juice and olive oil. Drizzle over the quinoa mixture.
5. Season with salt and pepper. Garnish with fresh cilantro. Serve this power bowl warm or chilled.

Nutritional Value (Amount per Serving):

Calories: 481; Fat: 17.9; Carb: 66.69; Protein: 17.8

Wild Mushroom Risotto

Prep Time: 10 Minutes   Cook Time: 25 Minutes   Serves: 4

Ingredients:

- 1 cup Arborio rice
- 4 cups vegetable or chicken broth, heated
- 1 cup mixed wild mushrooms, sliced
- 1/2 cup dry white wine
- 1/2 cup grated Parmesan cheese
- 2 tablespoons butter
- 1 onion, finely chopped
- 2 cloves garlic, minced

- Salt and pepper to taste

1. Select the 'Sear/Saute' function. Saute chopped onion and minced garlic at medium temperature until softened. Add sliced mushrooms and cook until browned.
2. Add Arborio rice to the pot. Stir to coat the rice with the mushroom mixture. Sear for 2 minutes.
3. Pour in the white wine, stirring until mostly evaporated.
4. Select the 'Slow Cook' function and add heated broth gradually, stirring occasionally. Cook on Low for 20 minutes or until rice is creamy and cooked.
5. Stir in Parmesan cheese and butter. Season with salt and pepper. Serve this creamy wild mushroom risotto hot.

Nutritional Value (Amount per Serving):

Calories: 538; Fat: 25.75; Carb: 65.82; Protein: 22.7

Lentil and Vegetable Stew with Barley

Prep Time: 15 Minutes   Cook Time: 30 Minutes   Serves: 4

Ingredients:

- 1 cup pearl barley
- 1 cup dried green or brown lentils, rinsed
- 1 onion, diced
- 2 carrots, diced
- 2 celery stalks, diced
- 4 cups vegetable broth
- 2 cloves garlic, minced
- 1 can (14 oz) diced tomatoes
- 1 teaspoon dried thyme
- Salt and pepper to taste

Directions:

1. Select the 'Sear/Saute' function. Saute diced onion, carrots, and celery at medium temperature until softened.
2. Stir in rinsed lentils, pearl barley, and minced garlic.
3. Pour in vegetable broth. Add diced tomatoes (with juice) and dried thyme. Stir well.
4. Select the 'Slow Cook' function and cook on Low for 25-30 minutes, or until lentils and barley are tender.
5. Season with salt and pepper to taste. Serve this hearty lentil and vegetable stew hot.

Nutritional Value (Amount per Serving):

Calories: 248; Fat: 0.95; Carb: 55.13; Protein: 8.03

Spinach and Feta Stuffed Bell Peppers with Quinoa

Prep Time: 20 Minutes   Cook Time: 25 Minutes   Serves: 4

Ingredients:

- 1 cup quinoa, cooked
- 4 bell peppers, halved and seeds removed
- 2 cups fresh spinach, chopped
- 1 cup feta cheese, crumbled
- 1/2 cup cherry tomatoes, diced
- 1/4 cup pine nuts, toasted
- 2 cloves garlic, minced
- 2 tablespoons olive oil
- Salt and pepper to taste

Directions:

1. Cook quinoa using the 'White Rice' function in the Ninja Foodi Cooker.
2. Cut bell peppers in half lengthwise. Remove seeds and membranes.
3. In a bowl, mix cooked quinoa, chopped spinach, feta cheese, diced cherry tomatoes, toasted pine nuts, minced garlic, olive oil, salt, and pepper.
4. Stuff each bell pepper half with the quinoa filling.
5. Arrange stuffed bell peppers in the cooker. Select the 'Slow Cook' function and cook on Low for 20-25 minutes, or until peppers are tender.
6. Serve these delicious spinach and feta stuffed bell peppers hot. Enjoy!

Nutritional Value (Amount per Serving):

Calories: 401; Fat: 23.27; Carb: 36.43; Protein: 14.15

Cajun Red Beans and Rice

Prep Time: 15 Minutes   Cook Time: 35 Minutes   Serves: 4

Ingredients:

- 1 cup long-grain white rice
- 2 cups water
- 1 can (15 oz) red kidney beans, drained and rinsed
- 1 onion, diced
- 1 bell pepper, diced
- 2 celery stalks, diced

- 3 cloves garlic, minced
- 1 teaspoon Cajun seasoning
- 1/2 teaspoon thyme
- 1 bay leaf
- 2 tablespoons vegetable oil
- Salt and pepper to taste
- Green onions for garnish

Directions:

1. Rinse white rice under cold water. In the Ninja Foodi Cooker, combine rice and water. Select the 'White Rice' function and cook for 15 minutes. Take out rice when done, and wash the cooker.
2. Select the 'Sear/Saute' function. Saute diced onion, bell pepper, and celery in vegetable oil at medium temperature until softened.
3. Stir in red kidney beans, minced garlic, Cajun seasoning, thyme, and bay leaf.
4. Add the rice to the pot with the beans and vegetables. Stir to combine.
5. Select the 'Slow Cook' function and cook on Low for an additional 15-20 minutes to allow flavors to meld.
6. Season with salt and pepper. Garnish with chopped green onions. Serve this flavorful Cajun red beans and rice hot.

Nutritional Value (Amount per Serving):

Calories: 370; Fat: 7.68; Carb: 65.71; Protein: 10.66

Lemon Garlic Quinoa with Roasted Vegetables

Prep Time: 20 Minutes   Cook Time: 25 Minutes   Serves: 4

Ingredients:

- 1 cup quinoa, rinsed
- 2 cups vegetable broth
- 1 zucchini, diced
- 1 bell pepper, sliced
- 1 cup cherry tomatoes, halved
- 2 tablespoons olive oil
- 2 cloves garlic, minced
- 1 lemon, juiced
- 1 teaspoon dried oregano
- Salt and pepper to taste
- Fresh parsley for garnish

Directions:

1. Rinse quinoa under cold water. In the Ninja Foodi Cooker, combine quinoa and vegetable broth. Select the 'White Rice' function and cook for 15 minutes.
2. While quinoa is cooking, toss diced zucchini, sliced bell pepper, and halved cherry tomatoes in olive oil.
3. In a large bowl, mix cooked quinoa, roasted vegetables, minced garlic,

lemon juice, and dried oregano.
4. Season with salt and pepper to taste. Garnish with fresh parsley.
5. Serve this lemon garlic quinoa with roasted vegetables warm.

Nutritional Value (Amount per Serving):

Calories: 241; Fat: 9.49; Carb: 33.26; Protein: 6.92

Blackened Shrimp and Rice Skillet

Prep Time: 15 Minutes   Cook Time: 20 Minutes   Serves: 4

Ingredients:

- 1 cup jasmine rice
- 1 pound large shrimp, peeled and deveined
- 2 tablespoons blackening seasoning
- 1 tablespoon olive oil
- 1 bell pepper, diced
- 1 onion, diced
- 1 cup corn kernels
- 1 can (14 oz) diced tomatoes, drained
- 2 cloves garlic, minced
- Fresh cilantro for garnish
- Lime wedges for serving

Directions:

1. In the Ninja Foodi Cooker, cook jasmine rice using the 'White Rice' function. Set aside.
2. Toss shrimp in blackening seasoning, ensuring they are evenly coated.
3. Select the 'Sear/Saute' function. Heat olive oil and saute diced bell pepper and onion at medium temperature. Add seasoned shrimp, corn, diced tomatoes, and minced garlic. Cook until shrimp are opaque.
4. Add the cooked jasmine rice to the skillet. Stir to combine with the shrimp and vegetables.
5. Season with additional blackening seasoning if desired. Garnish with fresh cilantro.
6. Serve this flavorful blackened shrimp and rice skillet hot with lime wedges.

Nutritional Value (Amount per Serving):

Calories: 209; Fat: 10.49; Carb: 32.73; Protein: 6.95

Stuffed Acorn Squash with Quinoa and Cranberries

Prep Time: 20 Minutes   Cook Time: 40 Minutes   Serves: 4

Ingredients:

- 2 acorn squash, halved and seeds removed
- 1 cup quinoa, cooked
- 1/2 cup dried cranberries
- 1/2 cup pecans, chopped
- 2 tablespoons maple syrup
- 1 teaspoon cinnamon
- 1/2 teaspoon nutmeg
- Salt and pepper to taste
- Greek yogurt for serving

Directions:

1. Cut acorn squash in half and remove seeds. Place in the Ninja Foodi Cooker and cook using the 'Sear/Saute' function at medium temperature until tender.
2. In a bowl, mix cooked quinoa, dried cranberries, chopped pecans, maple syrup, cinnamon, nutmeg, salt, and pepper.
3. Spoon the quinoa filling into the seared acorn squash halves.
4. Select the 'Slow Cook' function and cook on Low for an additional 15-20 minutes to allow flavors to meld.
5. Serve the stuffed acorn squash hot, topped with a dollop of Greek yogurt if desired.

Nutritional Value (Amount per Serving):

Calories: 391; Fat: 11.95; Carb: 64.91; Protein: 11.3

Spanish Chorizo and Saffron Rice

Prep Time: 15 Minutes   Cook Time: 25 Minutes   Serves: 4

Ingredients:

- 1 cup Arborio rice
- 2 cups chicken broth
- 1/2 cup dry white wine
- 1/2 cup Spanish chorizo, sliced
- 1 onion, finely chopped
- 2 cloves garlic, minced
- 1/4 teaspoon saffron threads
- 1/2 cup frozen peas
- Salt and pepper to taste
- Lemon wedges for serving

Directions:

1. Select the 'Sear/Saute' function. Saute sliced Spanish chorizo, chopped onion, and minced garlic at medium temperature until the onion is translucent.
2. Add Arborio rice to the pot. Saute for 2 minutes, stirring constantly.
3. Pour in the white wine and add saffron threads. Stir until the wine is

mostly evaporated.

4. Select the 'White Rice' function. Add chicken broth gradually, stirring occasionally. Cook for 20 minutes or until rice is creamy and cooked.
5. Stir in frozen peas. Season with salt and pepper to taste.
6. Serve this Spanish chorizo and saffron rice hot, with lemon wedges on the side.

Nutritional Value (Amount per Serving):

Calories: 512; Fat: 31.12; Carb: 22.77; Protein: 42.56

Southwest Quinoa Stuffed Peppers

Prep Time: 20 Minutes   Cook Time: 30 Minutes   Serves: 4

Ingredients:

- 1 cup quinoa, cooked
- 4 large bell peppers, halved and seeds removed
- 1 pound ground turkey or beef
- 1 cup black beans, drained and rinsed
- 1 cup corn kernels
- 1 cup diced tomatoes
- 1 teaspoon cumin
- 1 teaspoon chili powder
- Salt and pepper to taste
- Shredded cheese for topping
- Fresh cilantro for garnish

Directions:

1. Cook quinoa using the 'White Rice' function in the Ninja Foodi Cooker. Take out the quinoa when done, and wash the cooker.
2. In the cooker, select the 'Sear/Saute' function at medium temperature. Brown ground turkey or beef. Drain excess fat.
3. In a bowl, mix cooked quinoa, browned meat, black beans, corn, diced tomatoes, cumin, chili powder, salt, and pepper.
4. Stuff each bell pepper half with the quinoa mixture. Top with shredded cheese.
5. Saute the stuffed peppers until the cheese is melted and bubbly.
6. Garnish with fresh cilantro.
7. Serve these Southwest quinoa stuffed peppers hot.

Nutritional Value (Amount per Serving):

Calories: 539; Fat: 19.59; Carb: 51.72; Protein: 41.93

Pecan and Cranberry Wild Rice Pilaf

Prep Time: 15 Minutes   Cook Time: 40 Minutes   Serves: 4

Ingredients:

- 1 cup wild rice
- 3 cups vegetable broth
- 1/2 cup pecans, chopped
- 1/2 cup dried cranberries
- 1 onion, finely chopped
- 2 cloves garlic, minced
- 2 tablespoons olive oil
- 1 teaspoon dried sage
- Salt and pepper to taste
- Fresh parsley for garnish

Directions:

1. Rinse wild rice under cold water. In the Ninja Foodi Cooker, combine wild rice and vegetable broth. Select the 'Brown Rice' function and cook for 35-40 minutes.
2. While the rice is cooking, sear chopped pecans until fragrant. Set aside.
3. When the rice is done, take it out and set aside.
4. In the cooker, select the 'Sear/Saute' function. Saute chopped onion and minced garlic in olive oil at medium temperature until softened.
5. Combine the rice with sauteed onion and garlic. Add dried cranberries, toasted pecans, dried sage, salt, and pepper.
6. Select the 'Slow Cook' function and cook on Low for an additional 10 minutes to allow flavors to meld.
7. Garnish with fresh parsley. Serve this pecan and cranberry wild rice pilaf hot.

Nutritional Value (Amount per Serving):

Calories: 335; Fat: 16.26; Carb: 42.89; Protein: 7.88

Mushroom and Spinach Farro Risotto

Prep Time: 15 Minutes   Cook Time: 35 Minutes   Serves: 4

Ingredients:

- 1 cup farro
- 4 cups vegetable broth, heated
- 1 onion, finely chopped
- 2 cloves garlic, minced
- 1 cup cremini mushrooms, sliced
- 2 cups fresh spinach, chopped
- 1/2 cup Parmesan cheese, grated
- 2 tablespoons butter
- 1/4 cup dry white wine
- Salt and pepper to taste

Directions:

1. Select the 'Sear/Saute' function. Saute chopped onion and minced garlic at medium temperature until softened. Add sliced cremini mushrooms and cook until browned.

2. Stir in farro and saute for 2 minutes, allowing it to absorb the flavors.
3. Pour in the white wine, stirring until mostly evaporated.
4. Select the 'Slow Cook' function and gradually add heated vegetable broth, stirring occasionally. Cook on Low for 25-30 minutes or until farro is creamy and cooked.
5. Stir in chopped spinach, Parmesan cheese, and butter. Cook for an additional 5 minutes until spinach wilts.
6. Season with salt and pepper to taste. Serve this mushroom and spinach farro risotto hot.

Nutritional Value (Amount per Serving):

Calories: 156; Fat: 10.84; Carb: 9.6; Protein: 6.2

Mediterranean Bulgur Salad

Prep Time: 15 Minutes   Cook Time: 15 Minutes   Serves: 4

Ingredients:

- 1 cup bulgur
- 2 cups vegetable broth, heated
- 1 cucumber, diced
- 1 cup cherry tomatoes, halved
- 1/2 cup Kalamata olives, sliced
- 1/2 cup feta cheese, crumbled
- 1/4 cup red onion, finely chopped
- 3 tablespoons olive oil
- 2 tablespoons lemon juice
- 1 teaspoon dried oregano
- Salt and pepper to taste
- Fresh parsley for garnish

Directions:

1. In the Ninja Foodi Cooker, combine bulgur and heated vegetable broth. Select the 'White Rice' function and cook for 15 minutes.
2. In a large bowl, combine diced cucumber, halved cherry tomatoes, sliced Kalamata olives, crumbled feta, and finely chopped red onion.
3. Fluff the cooked bulgur with a fork. Add it to the bowl of vegetables and toss.
4. In a small bowl, whisk together olive oil, lemon juice, dried oregano, salt, and pepper.
5. Pour the dressing over the bulgur mixture. Toss until well combined.
6. Season with salt and pepper to taste. Garnish with fresh parsley. Serve this refreshing Mediterranean bulgur salad chilled.

Nutritional Value (Amount per Serving):

Calories: 222; Fat: 16.22; Carb: 16.27; Protein: 5.11

Lemon Garlic Butter Shrimp and Orzo

Prep Time: 15 Minutes   Cook Time: 20 Minutes   Serves: 4

Ingredients:

- 1 cup orzo pasta
- 1 pound large shrimp, peeled and deveined
- 4 tablespoons unsalted butter
- 4 cloves garlic, minced
- Zest and juice of 1 lemon
- 1/4 cup fresh parsley, chopped
- Salt and pepper to taste
- Grated Parmesan cheese for serving

Directions:

1. In the Ninja Foodi Cooker, cook orzo pasta according to package instructions. Drain and set aside.
2. Select the 'Sear/Saute' function. Melt butter in the cooker and saute minced garlic at medium temperature until fragrant. Add shrimp and cook until pink.
3. Stir in the cooked orzo to the shrimp. Add lemon zest, lemon juice, chopped fresh parsley, salt, and pepper. Toss until well combined.
4. Allow the flavors to meld on the 'Sear/Saute' function for an additional 2-3 minutes.
5. Serve this lemon garlic butter shrimp and orzo hot, with a sprinkle of grated Parmesan cheese on top.

Nutritional Value (Amount per Serving):

Calories: 167; Fat: 8.6; Carb: 18.18; Protein: 5.46

Quinoa and Vegetable Stir-Fry

Prep Time: 15 Minutes   Cook Time: 20 Minutes   Serves: 4

Ingredients:

- 1 cup quinoa, cooked
- 1 tablespoon vegetable oil
- 1 cup broccoli florets
- 1 bell pepper, sliced
- 1 carrot, julienned
- 1 zucchini, sliced
- 1 cup snap peas, trimmed
- 3 tablespoons soy sauce
- 1 tablespoon sesame oil
- 1 tablespoon rice vinegar
- 1 teaspoon ginger, minced
- 2 cloves garlic, minced
- Green onions for garnish
- Sesame seeds for garnish

Directions:

1. Cook quinoa using the 'White Rice' function in the Ninja Foodi Cooker. When ready, take it out and set aside.
2. In the cooker, heat vegetable oil using the 'Sear/Saute' function. Stir-

fry broccoli, bell pepper, carrot, zucchini, and snap peas at medium temperature until tender-crisp.

3. Add cooked quinoa to the stir-fried vegetables. In a bowl, mix soy sauce, sesame oil, rice vinegar, minced ginger, and minced garlic. Pour over the quinoa and vegetables. Toss to combine.
4. Allow the stir-fry to cook for an additional 2-3 minutes, ensuring the flavors meld.
5. Garnish with sliced green onions and sesame seeds. Serve this quinoa and vegetable stir-fry hot.

Nutritional Value (Amount per Serving):

Calories: 318; Fat: 14.04; Carb: 40.51; Protein: 9.17

Black Bean and Corn Stuffed Sweet Potatoes

Prep Time: 15 Minutes   Cook Time: 40 Minutes   Serves: 4

Ingredients:

- 4 medium-sized sweet potatoes
- 1 can (15 oz) black beans, drained and rinsed
- 1 cup corn kernels
- 1 bell pepper, diced
- 1/2 cup red onion, finely chopped
- 1 teaspoon ground cumin
- 1 teaspoon chili powder
- 1/2 teaspoon smoked paprika
- Salt and pepper to taste
- Avocado slices for garnish
- Fresh cilantro for garnish

Directions:

1. In the Ninja Foodi Cooker, sear sweet potatoes using the 'Sear/Saute' function at medium temperature until tender.
2. In a bowl, mix drained black beans, corn kernels, diced bell pepper, finely chopped red onion, ground cumin, chili powder, smoked paprika, salt, and pepper.
3. Cut a slit in each seared sweet potato and fluff the insides. Stuff each sweet potato with the black bean and corn mixture.
4. Allow the stuffed sweet potatoes to cook on the 'Slow Cook' function on Low for an additional 10-15 minutes to meld the flavors.
5. Garnish with avocado slices and fresh cilantro. Serve these black bean and corn stuffed sweet potatoes hot.

Nutritional Value (Amount per Serving):

Calories: 387; Fat: 9.07; Carb: 67.28; Protein: 14.48

Chapter 3: Poultry

Lemon Herb Seared Chicken

Prep Time: 30 Minutes   Cook Time: 2 Hours   Serves: 6

Ingredients:

- 1 whole roasting chicken (about 4-5 lbs)
- 2 lemons, sliced
- 4 cloves garlic, minced
- 2 tablespoons olive oil
- 1 tablespoon chopped fresh rosemary
- 1 tablespoon chopped fresh thyme
- Salt and pepper to taste

Directions:

1. Rub the chicken with olive oil, minced garlic, rosemary, and thyme.
2. Season the chicken with salt and pepper.
3. Stuff the cavity with lemon slices.
4. Place the chicken in the Ninja Foodi Cooker and sear for 2 hours at low temperature or until golden brown.
5. Let it rest for 15 minutes before carving.
6. Serve the lemon herb sear chicken with seared vegetables.

Nutritional Value (Amount per Serving):

Calories: 1567; Fat: 70.59; Carb: 185.49; Protein: 63.47

Teriyaki Pineapple Chicken Thighs

Prep Time: 25 Minutes   Cook Time: 1 Hour 30 Minutes   Serves: 5

Ingredients:

- 8 bone-in, skin-on chicken thighs
- 1 cup teriyaki sauce
- 1/2 cup pineapple juice
- 1/4 cup brown sugar
- 2 teaspoons grated ginger
- 1 teaspoon garlic powder
- Green onions for garnish (optional)

Directions:

1. In a bowl, mix teriyaki sauce, pineapple juice, brown sugar, grated ginger, and garlic powder.
2. Place chicken thighs in the Ninja Foodi Cooker.
3. Pour the teriyaki mixture over the chicken.
4. Set the cooker to Braise on Medium for 1.5 hours.
5. Garnish with chopped green onions if desired.
6. Serve the teriyaki pineapple chicken thighs over steamed rice.

Nutritional Value (Amount per Serving):

Calories: 1529; Fat: 140.53; Carb: 31.77; Protein: 34.6

Slow Cooker BBQ Pulled Turkey

Prep Time: 15 Minutes   Cook Time: 6 Hours   Serves: 8

Ingredients:

- 3 lbs turkey breast, boneless and skinless
- 1 cup BBQ sauce
- 1/4 cup apple cider vinegar
- 2 tablespoons brown sugar
- 1 tablespoon smoked paprika
- 1 teaspoon onion powder
- Slider buns for serving

Directions:

1. Season turkey breast with smoked paprika and onion powder.
2. Place the turkey in the Ninja Foodi Cooker.
3. In a bowl, mix BBQ sauce, apple cider vinegar, and brown sugar.
4. Pour the BBQ mixture over the turkey.
5. Set the cooker to Slow Cook on Low for 6 hours.
6. Shred the turkey with two forks.
7. Serve the BBQ pulled turkey on slider buns.

Nutritional Value (Amount per Serving):

Calories: 291; Fat: 12.26; Carb: 4.55; Protein: 38.67

Sear-Sauteed Lemon Butter Turkey Cutlets

Prep Time: 15 Minutes   Cook Time: 30 Minutes   Serves: 4

Ingredients:

- 1.5 lbs turkey cutlets
- 1/2 cup flour
- 1 teaspoon garlic powder
- 1 teaspoon onion powder
- 4 tablespoons butter
- Juice of 1 lemon
- 2 tablespoons chopped fresh parsley
- Salt and pepper to taste

Directions:

1. In a bowl, mix flour, garlic powder, and onion powder.
2. Dredge turkey cutlets in the flour mixture.
3. Using the Sear/saute function on Medium, heat butter in the Ninja Foodi

Cooker.

4. Sear turkey cutlets until golden brown on both sides.
5. Drizzle lemon juice over the cutlets.
6. Set the cooker to Keep Warm.
7. Garnish with chopped parsley before serving.

Nutritional Value (Amount per Serving):

Calories: 991; Fat: 87.36; Carb: 14.98; Protein: 34.62

Slow Cooked Orange Glazed Duck

Prep Time: 20 Minutes   Cook Time: 4 Hours   Serves: 4

Ingredients:

- 2 duck breasts
- 1 cup orange juice
- 1/4 cup soy sauce
- 2 tablespoons honey
- 1 teaspoon Chinese five-spice powder
- 2 cloves garlic, minced
- Green onions for garnish

Directions:

1. Score the skin of the duck breasts in a crisscross pattern.
2. In a bowl, mix orange juice, soy sauce, honey, five-spice powder, and minced garlic.
3. Place duck breasts in the Ninja Foodi Cooker.
4. Pour the orange glaze over the duck.
5. Set the cooker to Slow Cook on Low for 4 hours.
6. Garnish with chopped green onions before serving.

Nutritional Value (Amount per Serving):

Calories: 240; Fat: 6.57; Carb: 26.62; Protein: 18.86

Mediterranean Chicken Skewers

Prep Time: 25 Minutes   Cook Time: 20 Minutes   Serves: 4

Ingredients:

- 1.5 lbs boneless, skinless chicken breasts, cut into cubes
- 1 lemon, juiced
- 2 tablespoons olive oil
- 2 teaspoons dried oregano
- 1 teaspoon ground cumin
- 2 cloves garlic, minced
- Salt and pepper to taste

- Cherry tomatoes and red onion wedges for skewering

1. In a bowl, mix lemon juice, olive oil, oregano, cumin, minced garlic, salt, and pepper.
2. Marinate chicken cubes in the mixture for 15 minutes.
3. Skewer marinated chicken, cherry tomatoes, and red onion wedges alternately.
4. Use the Sear/saute function on Medium to cook skewers until chicken is cooked through.
5. Serve the Mediterranean chicken skewers over couscous or quinoa.

Nutritional Value (Amount per Serving):

Calories: 369; Fat: 16.63; Carb: 38.66; Protein: 16.31

Slow Cooked Cajun Turkey Stew

Prep Time: 20 Minutes   Cook Time: 6 Hours   Serves: 6

Ingredients:

- 2 lbs turkey thighs, boneless and skinless, cut into chunks
- 1 onion, diced
- 1 bell pepper, diced
- 2 celery stalks, chopped
- 3 cloves garlic, minced
- 1 can (14 oz) diced tomatoes
- 1 cup chicken broth
- 2 tablespoons Cajun seasoning
- 1 teaspoon dried thyme
- Salt and pepper to taste

Directions:

1. Season turkey chunks with Cajun seasoning, dried thyme, salt, and pepper.
2. Place turkey in the Ninja Foodi cooking pot.
3. Add diced onion, bell pepper, celery, minced garlic, diced tomatoes, and chicken broth.
4. Set the cooker to Slow Cook on Low for 6 hours.
5. Stir the stew occasionally during cooking.
6. Serve the Cajun turkey stew over cooked rice.

Nutritional Value (Amount per Serving):

Calories: 285; Fat: 10.23; Carb: 9.97; Protein: 36.13

Honey Sriracha Glazed Chicken Wings

Prep Time: 15 Minutes   Cook Time: 30 Minutes   Serves: 4

Ingredients:

- 2 lbs chicken wings
- 1/4 cup honey
- 2 tablespoons soy sauce
- 1 tablespoon Sriracha sauce
- 2 tablespoons melted butter
- 1 teaspoon garlic powder
- Sesame seeds and chopped green onions for garnish

Directions:

1. Set the Ninja Foodi Cooker the Sear/Saute function at medium temperature.
2. In a bowl, mix honey, soy sauce, Sriracha sauce, melted butter, and garlic powder.
3. Toss chicken wings in the honey Sriracha mixture.
4. Place wings in the cooker.
5. Sear for 25-30 minutes or until wings are crispy and cooked through.
6. Garnish with sesame seeds and chopped green onions before serving.

Nutritional Value (Amount per Serving):

Calories: 444; Fat: 16.77; Carb: 20.61; Protein: 51.23

Lemon Dill Grilled Chicken Breast

Prep Time: 20 Minutes   Cook Time: 15 Minutes   Serves: 4

Ingredients:

- 4 boneless, skinless chicken breasts
- Zest and juice of 2 lemons
- 3 tablespoons olive oil
- 2 tablespoons fresh dill, chopped
- 1 teaspoon garlic powder
- Salt and pepper to taste

Directions:

1. In a bowl, mix lemon zest, lemon juice, olive oil, chopped dill, garlic powder, salt, and pepper.
2. Marinate chicken breasts in the mixture for 15 minutes.
3. Set the cooker to the Sear/Saute function on Medium.
4. Sear chicken breasts for about 6-7 minutes per side or until fully cooked.
5. Let the chicken rest for 5 minutes before serving.

Nutritional Value (Amount per Serving):

Calories: 507; Fat: 23.6; Carb: 52.48; Protein: 21.99

Sear-Sauteed Coconut Lime Chicken Thighs

Prep Time: 25 Minutes   Cook Time: 30 Minutes   Serves: 5

Ingredients:

- 8 bone-in, skin-on chicken thighs
- 1 can (14 oz) coconut milk
- Zest and juice of 2 limes
- 2 tablespoons fish sauce
- 1 tablespoon brown sugar
- 1 teaspoon ground coriander
- Fresh cilantro for garnish

Directions:

1. Season chicken thighs with salt and pepper.
2. Using the Sear/saute function on Medium, brown chicken thighs on both sides.
3. In a bowl, mix coconut milk, lime zest, lime juice, fish sauce, brown sugar, and ground coriander.
4. Pour the coconut lime mixture over the chicken.
5. Set the cooker to Braise on Medium for 30 minutes.
6. Garnish with fresh cilantro before serving.

Nutritional Value (Amount per Serving):

Calories: 1590; Fat: 159.41; Carb: 9.49; Protein: 32.8

Moroccan Spiced Chicken Tagine

Prep Time: 30 Minutes   Cook Time: 2 Hours   Serves: 4

Ingredients:

- 4 chicken legs, skin-on
- 1 onion, finely chopped
- 2 carrots, sliced
- 1 cup dried apricots, halved
- 1 can (14 oz) chickpeas, drained and rinsed
- 2 teaspoons ground cumin
- 1 teaspoon ground coriander
- 1 teaspoon ground cinnamon
- 1 teaspoon paprika
- Salt and pepper to taste
- Fresh cilantro for garnish

Directions:

1. In a bowl, mix cumin, coriander, cinnamon, paprika, salt, and pepper.
2. Rub the spice mixture over the chicken legs.
3. In the Ninja Foodi Cooker, sauté chopped onions until softened using the

Sear/saute function on Medium.

4. Add chicken legs and brown on all sides.
5. Add carrots, apricots, and chickpeas to the pot.
6. Set the cooker to Braise on Low for 2 hours.
7. Garnish with fresh cilantro before serving.

Nutritional Value (Amount per Serving):

Calories: 509; Fat: 13.32; Carb: 40.22; Protein: 57.33

Teriyaki Grilled Turkey Burgers

Prep Time: 20 Minutes   Cook Time: 15 Minutes   Serves: 4

Ingredients:

- 1.5 lbs ground turkey
- 1/4 cup teriyaki sauce
- 2 tablespoons breadcrumbs
- 1 tablespoon soy sauce
- 1 teaspoon garlic powder
- 4 whole wheat burger buns
- Lettuce, tomato, and red onion for toppings

Directions:

1. In a bowl, mix ground turkey, teriyaki sauce, breadcrumbs, soy sauce, and garlic powder.
2. Form the mixture into burger patties.
3. Set the Ninja Foodi Cooker the Sear/Saute function on Medium.
4. Sear turkey burgers for about 7-8 minutes per side or until fully cooked.
5. Sear burger buns in the cooker.
6. Assemble burgers with lettuce, tomato, and red onion.

Nutritional Value (Amount per Serving):

Calories: 323; Fat: 13.97; Carb: 13.08; Protein: 36.7

Slow Cooked Creamy Garlic Parmesan Chicken

Prep Time: 15 Minutes   Cook Time: 4 Hours   Serves: 6

Ingredients:

- 2.5 lbs boneless, skinless chicken breasts
- 1 cup chicken broth
- 1 cup heavy cream
- 1 cup grated Parmesan cheese
- 4 cloves garlic, minced
- 1 teaspoon dried thyme
- Salt and pepper to taste

- Fresh parsley for garnish

Directions:

1. Season chicken breasts with salt, pepper, and dried thyme.
2. Place chicken in the Ninja Foodi Cooker.
3. In a bowl, mix chicken broth, heavy cream, grated Parmesan, and minced garlic.
4. Pour the creamy mixture over the chicken.
5. Set the cooker to Slow Cook on Low for 4 hours.
6. Garnish with fresh parsley before serving.

Nutritional Value (Amount per Serving):

Calories: 539; Fat: 25.63; Carb: 44.37; Protein: 31.74

Sear-Sauteed Buffalo Chicken Tenders

Prep Time: 15 Minutes   Cook Time: 15 Minutes   Serves: 4

Ingredients:

- 1.5 lbs chicken tenders
- 1/2 cup buffalo sauce
- 2 tablespoons melted butter
- 1 teaspoon garlic powder
- 1 teaspoon onion powder
- Blue cheese dressing for dipping
- Celery sticks for serving

Directions:

1. In a bowl, mix buffalo sauce, melted butter, garlic powder, and onion powder.
2. Coat chicken tenders in the buffalo mixture.
3. Using the Sear/saute function on Medium, cook chicken tenders until fully cooked.
4. Serve buffalo chicken tenders with blue cheese dressing and celery sticks.

Nutritional Value (Amount per Serving):

Calories: 619; Fat: 35.21; Carb: 46.98; Protein: 28.74

Lemon Garlic Butter Duck

Prep Time: 30 Minutes   Cook Time: 2 Hours 30 Minutes   Serves: 4

Ingredients:

- 1 whole duck (about 5 lbs)
- Zest and juice of 2 lemons
- 4 tablespoons melted butter
- 4 cloves garlic, minced
- 2 teaspoons dried thyme
- Salt and pepper to taste
- Fresh rosemary for garnish

Directions:

1. Set the Ninja Foodi Cooker to the Slow Cook function on High.
2. Rub the duck with lemon zest, melted butter, minced garlic, dried thyme, salt, and pepper.
3. Place the duck in the Ninja Foodi Cooker and slow cook for 2.5 hours.
4. Baste the duck with the pan juices occasionally.
5. Garnish with fresh rosemary before serving.

Nutritional Value (Amount per Serving):

Calories: 1169; Fat: 89.84; Carb: 12.56; Protein: 73.36

Garlic Herb Butter Seared Chicken

Prep Time: 30 Minutes   Cook Time: 30 Minutes   Serves: 4

Ingredients:

- 1 whole chicken (about 4-5 lbs)
- 1/2 cup unsalted butter, softened
- 4 cloves garlic, minced
- 1 tablespoon chopped fresh rosemary
- 1 tablespoon chopped fresh thyme
- Zest and juice of 1 lemon
- Salt and pepper to taste

Directions:

1. Set the Ninja Foodi Cooker to the Sear/Saute function on High.
2. In a bowl, mix softened butter, minced garlic, rosemary, thyme, lemon zest, and lemon juice.
3. Season the chicken with salt and pepper.
4. Rub the garlic herb butter mixture over and inside the chicken.
5. Place the chicken in the cooker and sear for 30 minutes or until the internal temperature reaches 165°F.
6. Baste the chicken with pan juices during cooking.
7. Let the chicken rest for 15 minutes before carving.

Nutritional Value (Amount per Serving):

Calories: 1194; Fat: 51.25; Carb: 103.34; Protein: 83.94

Thai Basil Chicken Stir-Fry

Prep Time: 20 Minutes   Cook Time: 15 Minutes   Serves: 4

Ingredients:

- 1.5 lbs boneless, skinless chicken thighs, thinly sliced
- 2 tablespoons soy sauce
- 1 tablespoon oyster sauce
- 1 tablespoon fish sauce
- 1 tablespoon sugar

- 2 tablespoons vegetable oil
- 4 cloves garlic, minced
- 1 cup fresh basil leaves
- Cooked jasmine rice for serving

Directions:

1. In a bowl, mix soy sauce, oyster sauce, fish sauce, and sugar.
2. Heat vegetable oil in the Ninja Foodi Cooker using the Sear/saute function on High.
3. Add minced garlic and sliced chicken, stir-frying until cooked through.
4. Pour the sauce over the chicken and stir to coat.
5. Add fresh basil leaves and continue to stir until wilted.
6. Serve the Thai basil chicken over jasmine rice.

Nutritional Value (Amount per Serving):

Calories: 397; Fat: 18.02; Carb: 41.85; Protein: 16.84

Lemon Pepper Sauted Cornish Hens

Prep Time: 25 Minutes   Cook Time: 45 Minutes   Serves: 4

Ingredients:

- 2 Cornish hens
- Zest and juice of 2 lemons
- 2 tablespoons olive oil
- 1 tablespoon black pepper
- 1 teaspoon garlic powder
- 1 teaspoon dried thyme
- Salt to taste

Directions:

1. Set the Ninja Foodi Cooker to the Sear/Saute function on Medium.
2. In a bowl, mix lemon zest, lemon juice, olive oil, black pepper, garlic powder, dried thyme, and salt.
3. Rub the lemon pepper mixture over the Cornish hens.
4. Sear the Cornish hens for about 20-25 minutes per side or until fully cooked.
5. Baste with the lemon pepper mixture during searing.
6. Let the Cornish hens rest for 10 minutes before serving.

Nutritional Value (Amount per Serving):

Calories: 1124; Fat: 37.08; Carb: 3.37; Protein: 182.21

Chapter 4: Beef, Pork and Lamb

Beef and Mushroom Stroganoff

Prep Time: 15 Minutes   Cook Time: 4 Hours   Serves: 4-6

Ingredients:

- 1.5 lbs beef sirloin, thinly sliced
- 1 onion, finely chopped
- 8 oz mushrooms, sliced
- 2 cloves garlic, minced
- 2 cups beef broth
- 1 cup sour cream
- 2 tablespoons flour
- Salt and pepper to taste
- Egg noodles, for serving

Directions:

1. Toss beef slices with flour, salt, and pepper.
2. In Ninja Foodi Cooker, sauté onions, garlic, and mushrooms at medium temperature until softened.
3. Add beef to the cooker, brown on all sides.
4. Pour in beef broth, set to Slow Cook for 4 hours on low.
5. Stir in sour cream just before serving.
6. Serve over cooked egg noodles.

Nutritional Value (Amount per Serving):

Calories: 531; Fat: 20.88; Carb: 54.29; Protein: 36.02

Maple Glazed Pork Tenderloin

Prep Time: 10 Minutes   Cook Time: 1 Hour   Serves: 4-6

Ingredients:

- 2 lbs pork tenderloin
- 1/2 cup maple syrup
- 2 tablespoons Dijon mustard
- 2 cloves garlic, minced
- 1 teaspoon thyme
- Salt and pepper to taste

Directions:

1. Set Ninja Foodi Cooker to the Sear/Saute function to Medium.
2. Season pork tenderloin with salt, pepper, and thyme.
3. Sear pork until browned on all sides.
4. In a bowl, mix maple syrup, Dijon mustard, and minced garlic.
5. Pour over pork and set the cooker to Braise function for 1 hour.
6. Slice and drizzle with the glaze.

Nutritional Value (Amount per Serving):

Calories: 351; Fat: 6.62; Carb: 22.77; Protein: 47.99

Pork and Black Bean Chili

Prep Time: 15 Minutes   Cook Time: 3 Hours   Serves: 4-6

Ingredients:

- 2 lbs pork shoulder, diced
- 1 onion, finely chopped
- 3 cloves garlic, minced
- 2 cans (15 oz each) black beans, drained and rinsed
- 1 can (14 oz) diced tomatoes
- 2 tablespoons chili powder
- 1 teaspoon cumin
- 1 teaspoon smoked paprika
- Salt and pepper to taste
- Sour cream and shredded cheese, for garnish

Directions:

1. Season pork with chili powder, cumin, smoked paprika, salt, and pepper.
2. Sear pork in Ninja Foodi Cooker at medium temperature until browned.
3. Add onions, garlic, black beans, and diced tomatoes.
4. Set the cooker to Slow Cook for 3 hours on low.
5. Top with sour cream and shredded cheese before serving.

Nutritional Value (Amount per Serving):

Calories: 647; Fat: 34.93; Carb: 27.21; Protein: 54.83

Grilled Lamb Kebabs

Prep Time: 20 Minutes   Cook Time: 15 Minutes   Serves: 4-6

Ingredients:

- 2 lbs lamb leg meat, cubed
- 1 red bell pepper, diced
- 1 red onion, diced
- 1/4 cup olive oil
- 2 tablespoons balsamic vinegar
- 2 teaspoons dried oregano
- Salt and pepper to taste
- Wooden skewers, soaked in water

Directions:

1. In a bowl, combine lamb, bell pepper, onion, olive oil, balsamic vinegar, oregano, salt, and pepper.
2. Thread onto soaked skewers.
3. Set Ninja Foodi Cooker to the Sear/Saute function at medium temperature.
4. Sear kebabs for about 15 minutes, turning occasionally.
5. Serve with a side of couscous or a fresh salad.

Nutritional Value (Amount per Serving):

Calories: 340; Fat: 26.44; Carb: 5.12; Protein: 19.54

Beef and Broccoli Stir-Fry

Prep Time: 15 Minutes   Cook Time: 20 Minutes   Serves: 4

Ingredients:

- 1.5 lbs beef flank steak, thinly sliced
- 2 cups broccoli florets
- 1/2 cup soy sauce
- 2 tablespoons hoisin sauce
- 2 tablespoons oyster sauce
- 1 tablespoon sesame oil
- 3 cloves garlic, minced
- 1 tablespoon cornstarch
- 2 tablespoons vegetable oil

Directions:

1. In a bowl, mix soy sauce, hoisin sauce, oyster sauce, sesame oil, and cornstarch.
2. Coat beef slices with the sauce.
3. Set Ninja Foodi Cooker to Sear/Saute on high.
4. Sear beef until browned; remove from Ninja Foodi.
5. Sear broccoli and garlic until tender-crisp.
6. Add beef back to the cooker; toss until well-coated.
7. Serve over steamed rice.

Nutritional Value (Amount per Serving):

Calories: 452; Fat: 24.88; Carb: 15.58; Protein: 39.89

Pork and Pineapple Skewers

Prep Time: 15 Minutes   Cook Time: 15 Minutes   Serves: 4-6

Ingredients:

- 2 lbs pork loin, cubed
- 1 pineapple, cut into chunks
- 1/4 cup soy sauce
- 2 tablespoons honey
- 1 tablespoon ginger, grated
- 2 cloves garlic, minced
- Salt and pepper to taste
- Wooden skewers, soaked in water

Directions:

1. In a bowl, mix soy sauce, honey, grated ginger, minced garlic, salt, and pepper.
2. Marinate pork cubes in the mixture.
3. Thread marinated pork and pineapple onto soaked skewers.
4. Set the Ninja Foodi Cooker to Sear/Saute function at medium temperature.
5. Sear skewers for about 15 minutes, turning occasionally.
6. Serve with rice or a side salad.

Nutritional Value (Amount per Serving):

Calories: 478; Fat: 22.45; Carb: 19.37; Protein: 47.89

Lamb Gyro Wraps

Prep Time: 20 Minutes   Cook Time: 30 Minutes   Serves: 4-6

Ingredients:

- 2 lbs lamb shoulder, thinly sliced
- 1 cucumber, diced
- 1 tomato, diced
- 1/2 cup red onion, thinly sliced
- 1/2 cup plain Greek yogurt
- 2 tablespoons olive oil
- 1 tablespoon lemon juice
- 2 teaspoons dried oregano
- Salt and pepper to taste
- Pita bread, for serving

Directions:

1. Season lamb slices with dried oregano, salt, and pepper.
2. Sear lamb in Ninja Foodi Cooker at medium temperature for 30 minutes until browned on all sides.
3. In a bowl, mix diced cucumber, tomato, red onion, Greek yogurt, olive oil, lemon juice, salt, and pepper.
4. Serve lamb in pita bread with the yogurt sauce.

Nutritional Value (Amount per Serving):

Calories: 441; Fat: 26.89; Carb: 7.1; Protein: 43.02

Teriyaki Beef Skewers

Prep Time: 15Minutes   Cook Time: 20inutes   Serves: 4-6

Ingredients:

- 1.5 lbs beef sirloin, cut into cubes
- 1 cup teriyaki sauce
- 1/4 cup brown sugar
- 2 tablespoons sesame oil
- 3 cloves garlic, minced
- 1 tablespoon ginger, grated
- 1 tablespoon cornstarch
- Wooden skewers, soaked in water

Directions:

1. In a bowl, mix teriyaki sauce, brown sugar, sesame oil, minced garlic, grated ginger, and cornstarch.
2. Marinate beef cubes in the mixture.
3. Thread marinated beef onto soaked skewers.
4. Set Ninja Foodi Cooker to Sear/Saute function at medium temperature.
5. Sear skewers for about 20 minutes, turning occasionally.
6. Serve over rice or noodles.

Nutritional Value (Amount per Serving):

Calories: 408; Fat: 20.62; Carb: 22.03; Protein: 31.71

Slow-Cooked Pork Carnitas

Prep Time: 20Minutes   Cook Time: 6 Hours   Serves: 4-6

Ingredients:

- 2 lbs pork shoulder, cubed
- 1 orange, juiced
- 2 limes, juiced
- 4 cloves garlic, minced
- 1 teaspoon cumin
- 1 teaspoon chili powder
- 1 teaspoon oregano
- Salt and pepper to taste
- Corn tortillas, for serving

Directions:

1. In a bowl, combine pork, orange juice, lime juice, minced garlic, cumin, chili powder, oregano, salt, and pepper.
2. Set Ninja Foodi Cooker to Slow Cook for 6 hours on low.
3. Shred pork using forks.
4. Serve pork carnitas in corn tortillas with your favorite toppings.

Nutritional Value (Amount per Serving):

Calories: 545; Fat: 32.65; Carb: 13.68; Protein: 46.93

Beef and Vegetable Kabobs

Prep Time: 20 Minutes   Cook Time: 15 Minutes   Serves: 4-6

Ingredients:

- 1.5 lbs beef sirloin, cut into chunks
- 1 zucchini, sliced
- 1 bell pepper, diced
- 1 red onion, cut into wedges
- 2 tablespoons olive oil
- 2 cloves garlic, minced
- 1 tablespoon balsamic vinegar
- 1 teaspoon dried rosemary
- Salt and pepper to taste
- Wooden skewers, soaked in water

Directions:

1. In a bowl, mix olive oil, minced garlic, balsamic vinegar, dried rosemary, salt, and pepper.
2. Marinate beef chunks and vegetables in the mixture.
3. Thread marinated beef and vegetables onto soaked skewers.
4. Set Ninja Foodi Cooker to Sear/Saute function at medium temperature.
5. Sear kabobs for about 15 minutes, turning occasionally.
6. Serve with a side of couscous or a fresh salad.

Calories: 326; Fat: 20.63; Carb: 4.8; Protein: 28.9

Honey Garlic Pork Chops

Prep Time: 15 Minutes   Cook Time: 25 Minutes   Serves: 4

Ingredients:

- 4 pork chops
- 1/4 cup honey
- 3 tablespoons soy sauce
- 2 tablespoons ketchup
- 2 cloves garlic, minced
- 1 teaspoon ginger, grated
- 1 tablespoon vegetable oil
- Green onions, chopped, for garnish

Directions:

1. In a bowl, mix honey, soy sauce, ketchup, minced garlic, and grated ginger.
2. Season pork chops with salt and pepper.
3. Set Ninja Foodi Cooker to the Sear/Saute function at medium temperature with vegetable oil.
4. Sear pork chops until golden brown.
5. Pour the honey garlic sauce over the pork chops and sear for an additional 10 minutes.
6. Garnish with chopped green onions and serve with rice.

Nutritional Value (Amount per Serving):

Calories: 473; Fat: 23.03; Carb: 24.37; Protein: 41.49

Lamb Chops with Mint Sauce

Prep Time: 15 Minutes   Cook Time: 20 Minutes   Serves: 4-6

Ingredients:

- 8 lamb chops
- 1/4 cup fresh mint, chopped
- 2 tablespoons olive oil
- 2 tablespoons red wine vinegar
- 1 teaspoon honey
- 2 cloves garlic, minced
- Salt and pepper to taste

Directions:

1. In a bowl, mix fresh mint, olive oil, red wine vinegar, honey, minced garlic, salt, and pepper.
2. Coat lamb chops with the mint sauce.
3. Set Ninja Foodi Cooker to Sear/Saute function at medium temperature.
4. Sear lamb chops for 20 minutes.

5. Drizzle with extra mint sauce before serving.

Calories: 848; Fat: 43.74; Carb: 2.43; Protein: 111.03

Spicy Korean Beef Stir-Fry

Prep Time: 15 Minutes   Cook Time: 20 Minutes   Serves: 4-6

Ingredients:

- 1.5 lbs beef flank steak, thinly sliced
- 1/2 cup soy sauce
- 3 tablespoons gochujang (Korean red pepper paste)
- 2 tablespoons sesame oil
- 1 tablespoon sugar
- 3 cloves garlic, minced
- 1 tablespoon vegetable oil
- Green onions, sliced, for garnish

Directions:

1. In a bowl, mix soy sauce, gochujang, sesame oil, sugar, and minced garlic.
2. Coat beef slices with the sauce.
3. Set Ninja Foodi Cooker to Sear/Saute on high with vegetable oil.
4. Sear beef for 20 minutes or until browned; remove it from the pot.
5. Garnish with sliced green onions before serving.

Nutritional Value (Amount per Serving):

Calories: 345; Fat: 19.62; Carb: 9.4; Protein: 31.26

Moroccan Lamb Tagine

Prep Time: 25 Minutes   Cook Time: 2 Hours   Serves: 4-6

Ingredients:

- 2 lbs lamb stew meat, cubed
- 1 onion, chopped
- 2 carrots, sliced
- 1 zucchini, diced
- 3 tablespoons tomato paste
- 1 cup dried apricots, chopped
- 1 teaspoon cumin
- 1 teaspoon coriander
- 1 teaspoon cinnamon
- Salt and pepper to taste
- Fresh cilantro, chopped, for garnish

Directions:

1. In Ninja Foodi Cooker, sauté onions at low temperature until softened.
2. Add lamb and brown on all sides.

3. Stir in carrots, zucchini, tomato paste, dried apricots, cumin, coriander, cinnamon, salt, and pepper.
4. Set cooker to Slow Cook for 2 hours on Low.
5. Garnish with chopped fresh cilantro before serving.

Nutritional Value (Amount per Serving):

Calories: 309; Fat: 15.93; Carb: 22.01; Protein: 20.88

Beef and Vegetable Stir-Fry with Black Bean Sauce

Prep Time: 15 Minutes   Cook Time: 20 Minutes   Serves: 4-6

Ingredients:

- 1.5 lbs beef sirloin, thinly sliced
- 2 cups broccoli florets
- 1 red bell pepper, sliced
- 1 cup snap peas, trimmed
- 1/4 cup black bean sauce
- 2 tablespoons soy sauce
- 1 tablespoon oyster sauce
- 1 tablespoon sesame oil
- 2 cloves garlic, minced
- 1 tablespoon vegetable oil

Directions:

1. In a bowl, mix black bean sauce, soy sauce, oyster sauce, and sesame oil.
2. Coat beef slices with the sauce.
3. Set Ninja Foodi Cooker to Sear/Saute on high with vegetable oil.
4. Sear beef until browned; remove from cooker.
5. Sear vegetables until tender-crisp.
6. Add beef back to the cooker; toss until well-coated.
7. Serve over steamed rice.

Nutritional Value (Amount per Serving):

Calories: 348; Fat: 22.45; Carb: 5.22; Protein: 29.75

Greek Lamb Souvlaki

Prep Time: 25 Minutes   Cook Time: 15 Minutes   Serves: 4-6

Ingredients:

- 2 lbs lamb leg, cut into cubes
- 1 lemon, juiced
- 1/4 cup olive oil
- 2 teaspoons dried oregano
- 3 cloves garlic, minced
- Salt and pepper to taste
- Tzatziki sauce, for serving
- Pita bread, for serving

Directions:

1. In a bowl, mix lemon juice, olive oil, dried oregano, minced garlic, salt, and pepper.

2. Marinate lamb cubes in the mixture.
3. Thread marinated lamb onto soaked skewers.
4. Set Ninja Foodi Cooker to Sear/Saute function at medium temperature.
5. Sear skewers for about 15 minutes, turning occasionally.
6. Serve with tzatziki sauce and pita bread.

Nutritional Value (Amount per Serving):

Calories: 365; Fat: 20.52; Carb: 5.89; Protein: 37.63

Pork and Vegetable Teriyaki Stir-Fry

Prep Time: 15 Minutes   Cook Time: 20 Minutes   Serves: 4-5

Ingredients:

- 1.5 lbs pork tenderloin, thinly sliced
- 2 cups mixed vegetables (bell peppers, broccoli, snow peas)
- 1/4 cup teriyaki sauce
- 2 tablespoons soy sauce
- 1 tablespoon honey
- 2 cloves garlic, minced
- 1 tablespoon vegetable oil

Directions:

1. In a bowl, mix teriyaki sauce, soy sauce, honey, and minced garlic.
2. Coat pork slices with the sauce.
3. Set Ninja Foodi to Sear/Saute on high with vegetable oil.
4. Sear pork until browned; remove from cooker.
5. Sear mixed vegetables until tender-crisp.
6. Add pork back to the cooker; toss until well-coated.
7. Serve over steamed rice.

Nutritional Value (Amount per Serving):

Calories: 293; Fat: 8.67; Carb: 15.07; Protein: 37.05

Moroccan Beef Tagine with Apricots

Prep Time: 20 Minutes   Cook Time: 2 Hours   Serves: 4-6

Ingredients:

- 2 lbs beef stew meat, cubed
- 1 onion, chopped
- 2 carrots, sliced
- 1 cup dried apricots, halved

- 3 tablespoons tomato paste
- 1 teaspoon ground cumin
- 1 teaspoon ground coriander
- 1 teaspoon ground cinnamon
- Salt and pepper to taste
- Fresh cilantro, chopped, for garnish

Directions:

1. In Ninja Foodi Cooker, sauté onions at low temperature until softened.
2. Add beef and brown on all sides.
3. Stir in carrots, dried apricots, tomato paste, cumin, coriander, cinnamon, salt, and pepper.
4. Set cooker to Slow Cook for 2 hours on Low.
5. Garnish with chopped fresh cilantro before serving.

Nutritional Value (Amount per Serving):

Calories: 236; Fat: 15.57; Carb: 24.62; Protein: 2.47

Chapter 5: Fish and Seafood

Coconut Lime Tilapia

Prep Time: 10 Minutes   Cook Time: 15 Minutes   Serves: 4

Ingredients:

- 4 tilapia fillets
- 1/2 cup coconut milk
- Zest and juice of 2 limes
- 2 tablespoons fresh cilantro, chopped
- 1 teaspoon ground cumin
- Salt and black pepper to taste
- Shredded coconut for garnish

Directions:

1. Set your Ninja Foodi Cooker to the "Sear/Saute" function on medium heat.
2. In a bowl, mix coconut milk, lime zest, lime juice, chopped cilantro, ground cumin, salt, and black pepper.
3. Sear tilapia fillets for 2-3 minutes on each side until lightly browned.
4. Pour the coconut lime sauce over the tilapia.
5. Reduce heat to low, cover, and braise for an additional 5-7 minutes until the fish is cooked through.
6. Sprinkle shredded coconut over the tilapia.
7. Plate the tilapia and drizzle with additional sauce. Serve with rice or your favorite side.

Nutritional Value (Amount per Serving):

Calories: 202; Fat: 9.38; Carb: 6.74; Protein: 24.77

Mediterranean Seared Swordfish

Prep Time: 15 Minutes   Cook Time: 12 Minutes   Serves: 4

Ingredients:

- 4 swordfish steaks
- 1/4 cup olive oil
- 2 tablespoons lemon juice
- 3 cloves garlic, minced
- 1 teaspoon dried oregano
- 1 teaspoon dried thyme
- Salt and black pepper to taste
- Cherry tomatoes and olives for garnish

Directions:

1. Set your Ninja Foodi Cooker to the "Sear/Saute" function on medium-high heat.
2. In a bowl, combine olive oil, lemon juice, minced garlic, dried oregano, dried thyme, salt, and black pepper. Marinate swordfish for 15 minutes.

3. Sear swordfish steaks for 5-6 minutes on each side until they are charred and cooked through.
4. Top with cherry tomatoes and olives.
5. Plate the swordfish steaks and serve with a squeeze of lemon.

Nutritional Value (Amount per Serving):

Calories: 625; Fat: 46.3; Carb: 2.88; Protein: 46.83

Shrimp and Broccoli Stir-Fry

Prep Time: 15 Minutes   Cook Time: 10 Minutes   Serves: 4

Ingredients:

- 1.5 pounds large shrimp, peeled and deveined
- 2 cups broccoli florets
- 3 tablespoons soy sauce
- 2 tablespoons oyster sauce
- 1 tablespoon hoisin sauce
- 1 tablespoon sesame oil
- 2 cloves garlic, minced
- 1 tablespoon grated ginger
- Green onions for garnish

Directions:

1. Set your Ninja Foodi Cooker to the "Sear/Saute" function on medium-high heat.
2. Sear shrimp for 2-3 minutes until they start to turn pink.
3. Add broccoli florets and continue searing for an additional 3-4 minutes until shrimp are cooked and broccoli is tender-crisp.
4. In a small bowl, mix soy sauce, oyster sauce, hoisin sauce, sesame oil, minced garlic, and grated ginger.
5. Pour the sauce over the shrimp and broccoli, tossing to coat evenly.
6. Garnish with chopped green onions.
7. Plate the shrimp and broccoli stir-fry and serve over rice or noodles.

Nutritional Value (Amount per Serving):

Calories: 133; Fat: 6.18; Carb: 16.97; Protein: 3.53

Lemon Dill Braised Cod

Prep Time: 10 Minutes   Cook Time: 20 Minutes   Serves: 4

Ingredients:

- 4 cod fillets
- 2 tablespoons olive oil

- Zest and juice of 1 lemon
- 2 tablespoons fresh dill, chopped
- 1 teaspoon garlic powder
- Salt and black pepper to taste
- Lemon slices for garnish

Directions:

1. Set your Ninja Foodi Cooker to the "Braise" function at medium temperature.
2. Brush cod fillets with olive oil and place them in the cooker.
3. Sprinkle lemon zest, lemon juice, chopped dill, garlic powder, salt, and black pepper over the cod.
4. Close the lid and braise for 15-18 minutes until the cod is flaky.
5. Garnish with lemon slices.
6. Plate the baked cod and serve hot.

Nutritional Value (Amount per Serving):

Calories: 162; Fat: 7.79; Carb: 5.1; Protein: 18.68

Spicy Cajun Catfish

Prep Time: 15 Minutes   Cook Time: 18 Minutes   Serves: 4

Ingredients:

- 4 catfish fillets
- 2 tablespoons Cajun seasoning
- 1 tablespoon olive oil
- 2 tablespoons hot sauce
- 1 tablespoon Worcestershire sauce
- 1 teaspoon smoked paprika
- Salt to taste
- Lemon wedges for serving

Directions:

1. Set your Ninja Foodi Cooker to the "Sear/Saute" function on medium-high heat.
2. Rub Cajun seasoning onto both sides of catfish fillets. Drizzle with olive oil, hot sauce, Worcestershire sauce, smoked paprika, and salt. Marinate for 10 minutes.
3. Sear catfish fillets for 3-4 minutes on each side until they are blackened and cooked through.
4. Plate the catfish and serve with lemon wedges.

Nutritional Value (Amount per Serving):

Calories: 203; Fat: 7.99; Carb: 4.57; Protein: 26.4

Garlic Lemon Butter Lobster Tails

Prep Time: 15 Minutes   Cook Time: 20 Minutes   Serves: 4

Ingredients:

- 4 lobster tails, split
- 1/2 cup unsalted butter, melted
- 4 cloves garlic, minced
- Zest and juice of 2 lemons
- 1 tablespoon chopped fresh parsley
- Salt and black pepper to taste

Directions:

1. Set your Ninja Foodi Cooker to the "Sear/Saute" function on medium heat.
2. In a bowl, mix melted butter, minced garlic, lemon zest, lemon juice, chopped parsley, salt, and black pepper.
3. Sear lobster tails, shell side down, for 2-3 minutes. Flip and brush with the garlic lemon butter mixture.
4. Close the lid and cook for an additional 12-15 minutes until the lobster meat is opaque and cooked through.
5. Baste the lobster tails with the garlic lemon butter mixture during cooking.
6. Plate the lobster tails and drizzle with additional garlic lemon butter. Serve hot.

Nutritional Value (Amount per Serving):

Calories: 174; Fat: 15.79; Carb: 7.13; Protein: 2.54

Teriyaki Pineapple Glazed Salmon

Prep Time: 10 Minutes   Cook Time: 18 Minutes   Serves: 4

Ingredients:

- 4 salmon fillets
- 1/2 cup teriyaki sauce
- 1/4 cup pineapple juice
- 2 tablespoons soy sauce
- 2 tablespoons brown sugar
- 1 teaspoon grated ginger
- 1/2 teaspoon garlic powder
- Pineapple slices for garnish

Directions:

1. Set your Ninja Foodi Cooker to the "Sear/Saute" function on medium-high heat.
2. In a bowl, mix teriyaki sauce, pineapple juice, soy sauce, brown sugar, grated ginger, and garlic powder.
3. Sear salmon fillets for 2-3 minutes on each side.
4. Pour the teriyaki pineapple glaze over the salmon.
5. Reduce heat to low, cover, and braise for an additional 12-15 minutes until the salmon is cooked through.
6. Garnish with pineapple slices.
7. Plate the salmon and drizzle with extra teriyaki pineapple glaze. Serve with rice or vegetables.

Nutritional Value (Amount per Serving):

Calories: 166; Fat: 5.54; Carb: 13.83; Protein: 14.59

Mediterranean Seafood Paella

Prep Time: 20 Minutes   Cook Time: 30 Minutes   Serves: 4

Ingredients:

- 1 cup Arborio rice
- 1/2 pound large shrimp, peeled and deveined
- 1/2 pound mussels, cleaned and debearded
- 1/2 pound squid, cleaned and sliced
- 1/2 cup diced tomatoes
- 1/2 cup chopped bell peppers
- 1/4 cup frozen peas
- 3 cloves garlic, minced
- 1 teaspoon saffron threads (optional)
- 2 teaspoons smoked paprika
- 4 cups seafood or chicken broth
- Lemon wedges for serving

Directions:

1. Set your Ninja Foodi Cooker to the "Saute" function on medium heat.
2. Saute garlic, bell peppers, and diced tomatoes until softened.
3. Add Arborio rice, saffron threads (if using), and smoked paprika. Stir to coat the rice.
4. Add shrimp, mussels, squid, and frozen peas.
5. Pour in seafood or chicken broth and stir well.
6. Close the lid and braise for 20-25 minutes until the rice is cooked, and the seafood is tender.
7. Plate the paella and serve with lemon wedges.

Nutritional Value (Amount per Serving):

Calories: 235; Fat: 9.09; Carb: 25.03; Protein: 22.34

Blackened Tuna Steaks

Prep Time: 10 Minutes   Cook Time: 10 Minutes   Serves: 4

Ingredients:

- 4 tuna steaks
- 2 tablespoons blackening seasoning
- 2 tablespoons olive oil
- 1 tablespoon soy sauce
- 1 teaspoon lemon juice
- 1/2 teaspoon cayenne pepper (optional)

- Lemon wedges for serving

1. Set your Ninja Foodi Cooker to the "Sear/Saute" function on medium-high heat.
2. Rub blackening seasoning onto both sides of tuna steaks.
3. Sear tuna steaks for 2-3 minutes on each side until they are blackened on the outside and pink in the center.
4. In a bowl, mix olive oil, soy sauce, lemon juice, and cayenne pepper (if using).
5. Drizzle the sauce over the blackened tuna steaks.
6. Plate the tuna steaks and serve with lemon wedges.

Nutritional Value (Amount per Serving):

Calories: 583; Fat: 40.27; Carb: 4.51; Protein: 46.93

Lemon Garlic Butter Clams

Prep Time: 15 Minutes   Cook Time: 10 Minutes   Serves: 4

Ingredients:

- 2 pounds fresh clams, cleaned
- 4 tablespoons unsalted butter
- 4 cloves garlic, minced
- Zest and juice of 1 lemon
- 1/4 cup chopped fresh parsley
- 1/2 cup dry white wine
- Crushed red pepper flakes (optional)
- Crusty bread for serving

Directions:

1. Set your Ninja Foodi Cooker to the "Sear/Saute" function on medium heat.
2. Saute minced garlic in butter until fragrant.
3. Add cleaned clams to the cooker.
4. Pour white wine over the clams, ensuring they are well-coated.
5. Close the lid and braise for 5-7 minutes until the clams open.
6. Add lemon zest, lemon juice, and chopped parsley. Toss to combine.
7. Plate the clams and broth in bowls, sprinkle with optional red pepper flakes, and serve with crusty bread.

Nutritional Value (Amount per Serving):

Calories: 250; Fat: 11.45; Carb: 31.71; Protein: 5.99

Honey Mustard Glazed Grilled Shrimp Skewers

Prep Time: 15 Minutes   Cook Time: 10 Minutes   Serves: 4

Ingredients:

- 1.5 pounds large shrimp, peeled and deveined
- 1/4 cup honey
- 2 tablespoons Dijon mustard
- 1 tablespoon whole grain mustard
- 2 tablespoons olive oil
- 2 cloves garlic, minced
- Salt and black pepper to taste
- Wooden skewers, soaked in water

Directions:

1. Set your Ninja Foodi Cooker to the "Sear/Saute" function on medium-high heat.
2. In a bowl, combine honey, Dijon mustard, whole grain mustard, olive oil, minced garlic, salt, and black pepper. Add shrimp and marinate for 10-15 minutes.
3. Thread marinated shrimp onto soaked wooden skewers.
4. Sear shrimp skewers for 2-3 minutes on each side until they are opaque and lightly charred.
5. Plate the shrimp skewers and drizzle with extra honey mustard glaze. Serve with a side salad or rice.

Nutritional Value (Amount per Serving):

Calories: 162; Fat: 7.36; Carb: 24.51; Protein: 1.93

Cilantro Lime Mahi-Mahi Tacos

Prep Time: 20 Minutes   Cook Time: 15 Minutes   Serves: 4

Ingredients:

- 4 Mahi-Mahi fillets
- 1/4 cup fresh lime juice
- 2 tablespoons olive oil
- 3 cloves garlic, minced
- 1 teaspoon ground cumin
- 1 teaspoon chili powder
- Salt and black pepper to taste
- 8 small corn tortillas
- Cabbage slaw (shredded cabbage, cilantro, lime juice)
- Avocado slices for garnish

Directions:

1. Set your Ninja Foodi Cooker to the "Sear/Saute" function on medium-high

heat.

2. In a bowl, combine lime juice, olive oil, minced garlic, ground cumin, chili powder, salt, and black pepper. Marinate Mahi-Mahi fillets for 15-20 minutes.
3. Sear Mahi-Mahi fillets for 2-3 minutes on each side until cooked through.
4. In the cooker, warm corn tortillas for 1-2 minutes.
5. Place Mahi-Mahi on tortillas, top with cabbage slaw, and garnish with avocado slices.
6. Serve the tacos with lime wedges on the side.

Nutritional Value (Amount per Serving):

Calories: 509; Fat: 31.07; Carb: 37.45; Protein: 24.27

Creamy Garlic Parmesan Scallops

Prep Time: 15 Minutes   Cook Time: 10 Minutes   Serves: 4

Ingredients:

- 1 pound sea scallops
- 2 tablespoons olive oil
- 4 cloves garlic, minced
- 1/2 cup heavy cream
- 1/4 cup grated Parmesan cheese
- Salt and black pepper to taste
- Chopped fresh parsley for garnish

Directions:

1. Set your Ninja Foodi Cooker to the "Sear/Saute" function on medium heat.
2. Pat dry scallops and sear for 2-3 minutes on each side until golden brown.
3. Add minced garlic to the cooker and saute for 1-2 minutes.
4. Pour heavy cream over the scallops, scraping any brown bits from the bottom of the pot.
5. Stir in grated Parmesan cheese, salt, and black pepper. Continue cooking until the sauce is creamy.
6. Sprinkle chopped fresh parsley over the scallops.
7. Plate the scallops and drizzle with the creamy garlic Parmesan sauce. Serve with pasta or crusty bread.

Nutritional Value (Amount per Serving):

Calories: 278; Fat: 15.15; Carb: 10.43; Protein: 26.24

Thai Red Curry Shrimp

Prep Time: 15 Minutes   Cook Time: 20 Minutes   Serves: 4

Ingredients:

- 1.5 pounds large shrimp, peeled and deveined

- 2 tablespoons red curry paste
- 1 can (14 oz) coconut milk
- 1 tablespoon fish sauce
- 1 tablespoon brown sugar
- 1 red bell pepper, sliced
- 1 zucchini, sliced
- Fresh cilantro for garnish
- Cooked jasmine rice for serving

Directions:

1. Set your Ninja Foodi Cooker to the "Sear/Saute" function on medium heat.
2. In the cooker, combine red curry paste, coconut milk, fish sauce, and brown sugar. Stir well.
3. Add shrimp, sliced bell pepper, and zucchini to the curry base.
4. Close the lid and braise for 15-18 minutes until the shrimp are cooked through and vegetables are tender.
5. Garnish with fresh cilantro.

Nutritional Value (Amount per Serving):

Calories: ;274 Fat: 24.51; Carb: 13.98; Protein: 4.43

Lemon Herb Cod with Vegetables

Prep Time: 20 Minutes   Cook Time: 25 Minutes   Serves: 4

Ingredients:

- 4 cod fillets
- 1/4 cup olive oil
- Zest and juice of 2 lemons
- 2 teaspoons dried thyme
- 1 teaspoon dried rosemary
- 1 teaspoon garlic powder
- Salt and black pepper to taste
- 1 pound baby potatoes, halved
- 1 cup baby carrots
- Fresh parsley for garnish

Directions:

1. Set your Ninja Foodi Cooker to the "Braise" function at medium temperature.
2. Brush cod fillets with olive oil and place them in the cooker.
3. Sprinkle lemon zest, lemon juice, dried thyme, dried rosemary, garlic powder, salt, and black pepper over the cod.
4. Add halved baby potatoes and baby carrots around the cod fillets.
5. Close the lid and braise for 20-25 minutes until the cod is flaky and vegetables are tender.
6. Garnish with fresh parsley.
7. Plate the baked cod and vegetables. Serve hot.

Nutritional Value (Amount per Serving):

Calories: 303; Fat: 14.24; Carb: 23.88; Protein: 20.7

Garlic Herb Butter Seared Lobster Tails

Prep Time: 20 Minutes   Cook Time: 15 Minutes   Serves: 4

Ingredients:

- 4 lobster tails, split
- 1/2 cup unsalted butter, melted
- 4 cloves garlic, minced
- 2 tablespoons chopped fresh parsley
- 1 teaspoon dried tarragon
- 1 teaspoon lemon zest
- Salt and black pepper to taste
- Lemon wedges for serving

Directions:

1. Set your Ninja Foodi Cooker to the "Sear/Saute" function on medium heat.
2. In a bowl, combine melted butter, minced garlic, chopped parsley, dried tarragon, lemon zest, salt, and black pepper.
3. Sear lobster tails, shell side down, for 2-3 minutes. Flip and brush with the garlic herb butter mixture.
4. Close the lid and cook for an additional 10-12 minutes until the lobster meat is opaque and cooked through.
5. Baste the lobster tails with the garlic herb butter mixture during cooking.
6. Plate the lobster tails and drizzle with additional garlic herb butter. Serve hot with lemon wedges.

Nutritional Value (Amount per Serving):

Calories: 173; Fat: 15.78; Carb: 6.52; Protein: 2.57

Chapter 6: Vegetables and Sides

Lemon Herb Rice Pilaf

Prep Time: 10 Minutes   Cook Time: 20 Minutes   Serves: 4

Ingredients:

- 1 cup long-grain white rice
- 2 cups vegetable broth
- Zest and juice of 1 lemon
- 2 tablespoons fresh parsley, chopped
- 1 tablespoon olive oil
- Salt and pepper to taste

Directions:

1. Set the Ninja Foodi Cooker to "White Rice" mode.
2. Heat olive oil and sauté rice until lightly golden.
3. Pour in vegetable broth, lemon zest, and lemon juice. Stir in fresh parsley.
4. Allow the cooker to cook the rice until it reaches a fluffy texture.
5. Season with salt and pepper to taste. Fluff the rice and transfer to a serving dish. Serve and enjoy!

Nutritional Value (Amount per Serving):

Calories: 212; Fat: 3.75; Carb: 40.49; Protein: 3.62

Braised Brussels Sprouts with Balsamic Glaze

Prep Time: 15 Minutes   Cook Time: 25 Minutes   Serves: 4

Ingredients:

- 1 lb Brussels sprouts, trimmed and halved
- 2 tablespoons olive oil
- 3 tablespoons balsamic glaze
- 2 cloves garlic, minced
- Salt and pepper to taste
- Chopped toasted almonds for garnish (optional)

Directions:

1. Set the Ninja Foodi Cooker to "Braise" mode and select "Medium" temperature.
2. Heat olive oil and braise Brussels sprouts until lightly browned.
3. Stir in minced garlic and balsamic glaze. Allow it to braise for 5-7 minutes.
4. Season with salt and pepper. Garnish with toasted almonds if desired.
5. Transfer to a serving dish and serve as a delightful side.

Nutritional Value (Amount per Serving):

Calories: 133; Fat: 7.43; Carb: 15.22; Protein: 5.15

Sear-Sautéed Garlic Butter Asparagus

Prep Time: 10 Minutes   Cook Time: 15 Minutes   Serves: 4

Ingredients:

- 1 lb asparagus, trimmed
- 2 tablespoons unsalted butter
- 3 cloves garlic, minced
- Zest of 1 lemon
- Salt and pepper to taste
- Grated Parmesan for garnish (optional)

Directions:

1. Set the Ninja Foodi Cooker to "Sear/Saute" mode and select "Medium" temperature.
2. Add unsalted butter to the pot. Sear asparagus until slightly charred.
3. Stir in minced garlic and lemon zest. Sauté for an additional 2-3 minutes.
4. Season with salt and pepper. Garnish with grated Parmesan if desired.
5. Transfer to a serving dish and serve this flavorful asparagus dish.

Nutritional Value (Amount per Serving):

Calories: 94; Fat: 4.41; Carb: 9.88; Protein: 5.98

Slow Cooked Maple Glazed Carrots

Prep Time: 10 Minutes   Cook Time: 4 Hours   Serves: 6

Ingredients:

- 1 lb baby carrots
- 1/4 cup maple syrup
- 2 tablespoons unsalted butter
- 1 teaspoon ground cinnamon
- Salt to taste
- Fresh parsley for garnish (optional)

Directions:

1. In the cooker, combine baby carrots, maple syrup, unsalted butter, and ground cinnamon.
2. Set the cooker to "Slow Cook" mode and select the Low temperature. Cook for 4 hours, stirring occasionally.
3. Season with salt to taste. Garnish with fresh parsley if desired.
4. Transfer to a serving dish and serve these sweet and glazed carrots.

Nutritional Value (Amount per Serving):

Calories: 87; Fat: 2.72; Carb: 15.68; Protein: 0.8

Brown Rice and Vegetable Medley

Prep Time: 15 Minutes   Cook Time: 25 Minutes   Serves: 4

Ingredients:

- 1 cup brown rice
- 2 cups vegetable broth
- 1 tablespoon olive oil
- 1 onion, finely chopped
- 1 bell pepper, diced
- 1 zucchini, diced
- 1 carrot, shredded
- 1 teaspoon garlic powder
- Salt and pepper to taste
- Chopped fresh parsley for garnish (optional)

Directions:

1. Set the Ninja Foodi Cooker to "Brown Rice" mode.
2. Heat olive oil and sauté onions, bell pepper, zucchini, and carrot until softened.
3. Stir in brown rice and pour in vegetable broth. Add garlic powder, salt, and pepper.
4. Allow the cooker to cook the rice until tender.
5. Garnish with fresh parsley if desired. Transfer to a serving dish and enjoy this wholesome rice medley.

Nutritional Value (Amount per Serving):

Calories: 208; Fat: 4.61; Carb: 38.15; Protein: 4.45

Sear-Sautéed Lemon Garlic Green Beans

Prep Time: 10 Minutes   Cook Time: 15 Minutes   Serves: 4

Ingredients:

- 1 lb green beans, trimmed
- 2 tablespoons olive oil
- 2 cloves garlic, minced
- Zest of 1 lemon
- 1/4 cup sliced almonds
- Salt and pepper to taste

Directions:

1. Set the Ninja Foodi Cooker to "Sear/Saute" mode and select "Medium" temperature.
2. Add olive oil to the pot. Sear green beans until they are slightly browned.
3. Stir in minced garlic and lemon zest. Sauté for an additional 2-3 minutes.
4. Add sliced almonds and toast for 2-3 minutes until golden.

5. Season with salt and pepper. Transfer to a serving dish and enjoy this vibrant side!

Nutritional Value (Amount per Serving):

Calories: 94; Fat: 7.37; Carb: 7.3; Protein: 1.65

Slow Cooker Ratatouille

Prep Time: 20 Minutes   Cook Time: 4 Hours   Serves: 6

Ingredients:

- 1 eggplant, diced
- 1 zucchini, sliced
- 1 yellow squash, sliced
- 1 bell pepper, diced
- 1 onion, chopped
- 3 cloves garlic, minced
- 1 can (14 oz) crushed tomatoes
- 2 tablespoons tomato paste
- 1 teaspoon dried thyme
- Salt and pepper to taste
- Fresh basil for garnish

Directions:

1. In the cooker, combine eggplant, zucchini, yellow squash, bell pepper, onion, garlic, crushed tomatoes, tomato paste, thyme, salt, and pepper.
2. Set the cooker to "Slow Cook" mode and select the Low temperature. Cook for 4 hours.
3. Adjust seasoning if needed. Garnish with fresh basil.
4. Transfer to a serving dish and serve this hearty Ratatouille.

Nutritional Value (Amount per Serving):

Calories: 49; Fat: 0.34; Carb: 11.26; Protein: 2.05

Sear-Sautéed Parmesan Brussels Sprouts

Prep Time: 15 Minutes   Cook Time: 20 Minutes   Serves: 4

Ingredients:

- 1 lb Brussels sprouts, trimmed and halved
- 2 tablespoons olive oil
- 3 tablespoons grated Parmesan cheese
- 1 teaspoon garlic powder
- Salt and pepper to taste
- Lemon wedges for serving

Directions:

1. Set the Ninja Foodi Cooker to "Sear/Saute" mode and select "Medium" temperature.

2. Add olive oil to the pot. Sear Brussels sprouts until they are golden brown.
3. Sprinkle grated Parmesan and garlic powder over the Brussels sprouts. Sauté for an additional 2-3 minutes.
4. Season with salt and pepper. Transfer to a serving dish and serve with lemon wedges on the side.

Nutritional Value (Amount per Serving):

Calories: 134; Fat: 8.19; Carb: 13.13; Protein: 5.29

Brown Rice Pilaf with Mixed Vegetables

Prep Time: 15 Minutes   Cook Time: 25 Minutes   Serves: 6

Ingredients:

- 1 cup brown rice
- 2 cups vegetable broth
- 2 tablespoons olive oil
- 1 onion, finely chopped
- 1 carrot, diced
- 1 bell pepper, diced
- 1 cup frozen peas
- Salt and pepper to taste
- Fresh parsley for garnish

Directions:

1. Set the Ninja Foodi Cooker to "Brown Rice" mode.
2. Heat olive oil and sauté onions, carrots, bell pepper, and frozen peas until vegetables are tender.
3. Stir in brown rice and pour in vegetable broth. Add salt and pepper.
4. Allow the cooker to cook the rice until tender.
5. Garnish with fresh parsley. Transfer to a serving dish and enjoy this colorful rice pilaf.

Nutritional Value (Amount per Serving):

Calories: 164; Fat: 5.34; Carb: 26.4; Protein: 3.35

Sear-Sautéed Garlic Herb Mushrooms

Prep Time: 10 Minutes   Cook Time: 15 Minutes   Serves: 4

Ingredients:

- 1 lb mushrooms, cleaned and sliced
- 3 tablespoons butter
- 4 cloves garlic, minced
- 1 teaspoon dried thyme
- 1 teaspoon dried rosemary
- Salt and pepper to taste
- Chopped fresh parsley for garnish

Directions:

1. Set the Ninja Foodi Cooker to "Sear/Saute" mode and select "Medium"

temperature.

2. Add butter to the pot. Sear mushrooms until they release their moisture and become golden.
3. Stir in minced garlic, thyme, and rosemary. Sauté for an additional 2-3 minutes.
4. Season with salt and pepper. Garnish with chopped fresh parsley.
5. Transfer to a serving dish and serve these flavorful garlic herb mushrooms.

Nutritional Value (Amount per Serving):

Calories: 427; Fat: 9.93; Carb: 88.57; Protein: 11.83

Slow Cooked Butternut Squash Risotto

Prep Time: 15 Minutes   Cook Time: 4 Hours   Serves: 6

Ingredients:

- 2 cups Arborio rice
- 4 cups vegetable broth
- 1 butternut squash, peeled and diced
- 1 onion, finely chopped
- 2 cloves garlic, minced
- 1/2 cup grated Parmesan cheese
- 2 tablespoons butter
- Salt and pepper to taste
- Chopped sage for garnish

Directions:

1. In the cooker, combine Arborio rice, vegetable broth, butternut squash, onion, and garlic.
2. Set the cooker to "Slow Cook" mode and select the Low temperature. Cook for 4 hours, stirring occasionally.
3. Stir in Parmesan cheese and butter. Season with salt and pepper.
4. Garnish with chopped sage.
5. Transfer to a serving dish and serve this creamy butternut squash risotto.

Nutritional Value (Amount per Serving):

Calories: 247; Fat: 14.49; Carb: 34.37; Protein: 8.84

Sear-Sautéed Lemon Garlic Asparagus

Prep Time: 10 Minutes   Cook Time: 15 Minutes   Serves: 4

Ingredients:

- 1 lb asparagus, trimmed
- 2 tablespoons olive oil
- 3 cloves garlic, minced
- Zest of 1 lemon
- 1/4 cup sliced almonds
- Salt and pepper to taste

Directions:

1. Set the Ninja Foodi Cooker to "Sear/Saute" mode and select "Medium"

temperature.

2. Add olive oil to the pot. Sear asparagus until they are slightly browned.
3. Stir in minced garlic and lemon zest. Sauté for an additional 2-3 minutes.
4. Add sliced almonds and toast for 2-3 minutes until golden.
5. Season with salt and pepper. Transfer to a serving dish and enjoy this vibrant side!

Nutritional Value (Amount per Serving):

Calories: 93; Fat: 6.99; Carb: 7.05; Protein: 2.92

Slow Cooker Garlic Mashed Cauliflower

Prep Time: 15 Minutes   Cook Time: 4 Hours   Serves: 6

Ingredients:

- 1 large head cauliflower, chopped into florets
- 4 cloves garlic, minced
- 1/2 cup vegetable broth
- 1/4 cup cream cheese
- 2 tablespoons butter
- Salt and pepper to taste
- Chopped chives for garnish

Directions:

1. In the cooker, combine cauliflower florets, minced garlic, and vegetable broth.
2. Set the cooker to "Slow Cook" mode and select the Low temperature. Cook for 4 hours, stirring occasionally.
3. Mash the cooked cauliflower with a potato masher. Add cream cheese and butter, continue mashing until smooth.
4. Season with salt and pepper. Garnish with chopped chives.
5. Transfer to a serving dish and serve this creamy garlic mashed cauliflower.

Nutritional Value (Amount per Serving):

Calories: 81; Fat: 6.85; Carb: 4.18; Protein: 1.88

Braised Rosemary Potatoes

Prep Time: 15 Minutes   Cook Time: 25 Minutes   Serves: 4

Ingredients:

- 1.5 lbs baby potatoes, halved
- 2 tablespoons olive oil
- 2 teaspoons fresh rosemary, chopped

- 3 cloves garlic, minced
- 1 cup vegetable broth
- Salt and pepper to taste
- Chopped fresh parsley for garnish

Directions:

1. Set the Ninja Foodi Cooker to "Braise" mode and select "Medium" temperature.
2. Heat olive oil and braise baby potatoes until they start to brown.
3. Stir in chopped rosemary and minced garlic. Sauté for 2-3 minutes.
4. Pour vegetable broth over the potatoes. Cover and let it braise for 15-20 minutes or until potatoes are tender.
5. Season with salt and pepper. Garnish with fresh parsley.
6. Transfer to a serving dish and serve these aromatic rosemary potatoes.

Nutritional Value (Amount per Serving):

Calories: 207; Fat: 7.08; Carb: 33.3; Protein: 4.26

White Rice Pilaf with Mixed Vegetables

Prep Time: 15 Minutes   Cook Time: 20 Minutes   Serves: 4

Ingredients:

- 1 cup white rice
- 2 cups vegetable broth
- 2 tablespoons olive oil
- 1 onion, finely chopped
- 1 carrot, diced
- 1 bell pepper, diced
- 1 cup frozen corn
- Salt and pepper to taste
- Fresh cilantro for garnish

Directions:

1. Set the Ninja Foodi Cooker to "White Rice" mode.
2. Heat olive oil and sauté onions, carrots, bell pepper, and frozen corn until vegetables are tender.
3. Stir in white rice and pour in vegetable broth. Add salt and pepper.
4. Allow the cooker to cook the rice until tender.
5. Garnish with fresh cilantro. Transfer to a serving dish and enjoy this flavorful rice pilaf.

Nutritional Value (Amount per Serving):

Calories: 311; Fat: 7.65; Carb: 54.82; Protein: 5.47

Sear-Sautéed Honey Glazed Carrots

Prep Time: 10 Minutes   Cook Time: 15 Minutes   Serves: 4

Ingredients:

- 1 lb baby carrots
- 2 tablespoons butter
- 3 tablespoons honey
- 1 teaspoon ground cumin
- Salt and pepper to taste
- Chopped fresh parsley for garnish

Directions:

1. Set the Ninja Foodi Cooker to "Sear/Saute" mode and select "Medium" temperature.
2. Add butter to the pot. Sear baby carrots until they are slightly browned.
3. Drizzle honey over the carrots and sprinkle ground cumin. Sauté for an additional 3-5 minutes.
4. Season with salt and pepper. Garnish with chopped fresh parsley.
5. Transfer to a serving dish and serve these sweet and glazed carrots.

Nutritional Value (Amount per Serving):

Calories: 150; Fat: 6.16; Carb: 24.57; Protein: 1.6

Slow Cooked Quinoa and Black Bean Stew

Prep Time: 15 Minutes   Cook Time: 4 Hours   Serves: 6

Ingredients:

- 1 cup quinoa, rinsed
- 2 cups vegetable broth
- 1 can (15 oz) black beans, drained and rinsed
- 1 bell pepper, diced
- 1 onion, chopped
- 3 cloves garlic, minced
- 1 teaspoon ground cumin
- 1 teaspoon chili powder
- Salt and pepper to taste
- Avocado slices for garnish

Directions:

1. In the cooker, combine quinoa, vegetable broth, black beans, bell pepper, onion, garlic, cumin, and chili powder.
2. Set the cooker to "Slow Cook" mode and select the Low temperature. Cook for 4 hours, stirring occasionally.
3. Adjust seasoning with salt and pepper.
4. Garnish with avocado slices.
5. Transfer to a serving dish and enjoy this hearty quinoa and black bean stew.

Nutritional Value (Amount per Serving):

Calories: 273; Fat: 7.21; Carb: 42.85; Protein: 11.67

Mushroom Marsala with Barley

Prep Time: 20 Minutes   Cook Time: 4 Hours 15 Minutes   Serves: 6

Ingredients:

- 1-1/2 pounds baby portobello mushrooms, cut into 3/4-in. chunks
- 1 cup thinly sliced shallots
- 3 tablespoons olive oil
- 1/2 teaspoon minced fresh thyme
- 3/4 cup Marsala wine, divided
- 3 tablespoons reduced-fat sour cream
- 2 tablespoons all-purpose flour
- 1-1/2 teaspoons grated lemon zest
- 1/4 teaspoon salt
- 1/4 cup crumbled goat cheese
- 1/4 cup minced fresh parsley
- 2-1/2 cups cooked barley

Directions:

1. In the Ninja Foodi Cooker, combine mushrooms, shallots, olive oil and thyme. Add 1/4 cup Marsala wine.
2. Switch to the Slow Cook function.
3. Cook, covered, on low for 4 hours or until vegetables are tender.
4. Stir in sour cream, flour, lemon zest, salt and remaining 1/2 cup Marsala.
5. Cook, covered, on low for 15 minutes longer. Sprinkle with goat cheese and parsley.
6. Serve with hot cooked barley.

Nutritional Value (Amount per Serving):

Calories: 186; Fat: 9.94; Carb: 20.16; Protein: 5.6

Chapter 7: Snacks and Appetizers

BBQ Pulled Pork Sliders

Prep Time: 15 Minutes   Cook Time: 4 Hours   Serves: 8-10

Ingredients:

- 2 lbs pork shoulder, trimmed and cut into chunks
- 1 cup barbecue sauce
- 1/2 cup brown sugar
- 1/4 cup apple cider vinegar
- 1 teaspoon smoked paprika
- 1 teaspoon garlic powder
- Slider buns
- Coleslaw for topping

Directions:

1. In the Ninja Foodi Cooker, select the sear/sauté function, sear the pork shoulder chunks at medium temperature.
2. In a bowl, mix together barbecue sauce, brown sugar, apple cider vinegar, smoked paprika, and garlic powder.
3. Pour the sauce over the pork.
4. Cook on low on the slow cook function for 4 hours until the pork is tender and easily shredded.
5. Serve the pulled pork on slider buns with coleslaw.

Nutritional Value (Amount per Serving):

Calories: 415; Fat: 20.41; Carb: 30.37; Protein: 26.06

Creamy Spinach and Artichoke Dip

Prep Time: 15 Minutes   Cook Time: 1 Hour 30 Minutes   Serves: 6-8

Ingredients:

- 1 cup frozen chopped spinach, thawed and drained
- 1 can artichoke hearts, drained and chopped
- 1 cup cream cheese, softened
- 1/2 cup mayonnaise
- 1/2 cup sour cream
- 1 cup grated Parmesan cheese
- 2 cloves garlic, minced
- 1/2 teaspoon onion powder
- Tortilla chips or sliced baguette for dipping

Directions:

1. In the Ninja Foodi Cooker, combine spinach, artichoke hearts, cream

cheese, mayonnaise, sour cream, Parmesan cheese, minced garlic, and onion powder.
2. Stir until the mixture is well combined and heated through.
3. Transfer to the cooker using the slow cook function and cook on low for 1.5 hours.
4. Stir occasionally and serve the creamy dip with tortilla chips or sliced baguette.

Nutritional Value (Amount per Serving):

Calories: 276; Fat: 22.07; Carb: 11.02; Protein: 9.73

Buffalo Cauliflower Bites

Prep Time: 20 Minutes   Cook Time: 1 Hour 30 Minutes   Serves: 4-6

Ingredients:

- 1 medium cauliflower, cut into florets
- 1 cup buffalo sauce
- 1/2 cup melted butter
- 1 teaspoon garlic powder
- 1 teaspoon onion powder
- 1/2 teaspoon cayenne pepper (optional)
- Ranch or blue cheese dressing for dipping
- Celery sticks for serving

Directions:

1. In the Ninja Foodi Cooker, mix buffalo sauce, melted butter, garlic powder, onion powder, and cayenne pepper.
2. Add cauliflower florets and stir until they are well coated with the sauce.
3. Using the slow cook function, and cook on low for 1.5 hours.
4. Serve the buffalo cauliflower bites with ranch or blue cheese dressing and celery sticks.

Nutritional Value (Amount per Serving):

Calories: 353; Fat: 24.97; Carb: 31.31; Protein: 3.4

Hawaiian BBQ Meatballs

Prep Time: 15 Minutes   Cook Time: 2 Hours   Serves: 6-8

Ingredients:

- 1.5 lbs ground pork or beef
- 1 cup breadcrumbs
- 2 eggs
- 1 cup barbecue sauce

- 1/2 cup pineapple juice
- 1/4 cup soy sauce
- 2 tablespoons brown sugar
- 1 teaspoon garlic powder
- 1 teaspoon ginger, grated
- Sliced green onions for garnish

Directions:

1. In a bowl, combine ground meat, breadcrumbs, eggs, barbecue sauce, pineapple juice, soy sauce, brown sugar, garlic powder, and grated ginger.
2. Shape the mixture into meatballs and sear in the Ninja Foodi Cooker using the sear/sauté function at medium temperature until browned.
3. Switch to the slow cook function, cook on low for 2 hours.
4. Garnish with sliced green onions before serving.

Nutritional Value (Amount per Serving):

Calories: 630; Fat: 46.96; Carb: 23.39; Protein: 25.97

Loaded Nachos

Prep Time: 15 Minutes   Cook Time: 1 Hour 30 Minutes   Serves: 4-6

Ingredients:

- Tortilla chips
- 2 cups shredded Mexican cheese blend
- 1 lb ground beef or turkey, cooked and seasoned with taco seasoning
- 1 can black beans, drained and rinsed
- 1 cup diced tomatoes
- 1/2 cup sliced black olives
- 1/4 cup chopped green onions
- Sour cream and guacamole for topping

Directions:

1. In the Ninja Foodi Cooker on the sear/sauté function at medium temperature, layer tortilla chips, shredded cheese, cooked ground meat, black beans, tomatoes, and black olives.
2. Repeat layers until ingredients are used, ending with a layer of cheese on top.
3. Switch to the slow cook function and cook on low for 1.5 hours or until cheese is melted and bubbly.
4. Top with chopped green onions, sour cream, and guacamole before serving.

Nutritional Value (Amount per Serving):

Calories: 502; Fat: 24.82; Carb: 26.54; Protein: 43.98

Mediterranean Stuffed Mushrooms

Prep Time: 20 Minutes   Cook Time: 1 Hour 30 Minutes   Serves: 4-6

Ingredients:

- 24 large mushrooms, cleaned and stems removed
- 1 cup crumbled feta cheese
- 1/2 cup chopped Kalamata olives
- 1/4 cup sun-dried tomatoes, chopped
- 2 cloves garlic, minced
- 2 tablespoons fresh parsley, chopped
- Olive oil for brushing
- Salt and pepper to taste

Directions:

1. In a bowl, mix together feta cheese, Kalamata olives, sun-dried tomatoes, minced garlic, and fresh parsley.
2. Stuff each mushroom cap with the mixture.
3. Brush the mushrooms with olive oil and place them in the Ninja Foodi Cooker on the sear/sauté function at medium temperature.
4. Cook for 10 minutes, turning occasionally until mushrooms are browned.
5. Switch to the slow cook function and cook on low for an additional 1.5 hours.
6. Season with salt and pepper before serving.

Nutritional Value (Amount per Serving):

Calories: 181; Fat: 13.99; Carb: 8.52; Protein: 8.47

Cheesy Bacon Wrapped Jalapeños

Prep Time: 20 Minutes   Cook Time: 1 Hour 30 Minutes   Serves: 6-8

Ingredients:

- 12 fresh jalapeños, halved and seeds removed
- 1 cup cream cheese, softened
- 1 cup shredded cheddar cheese
- 12 slices bacon, halved
- Toothpicks

Directions:

1. In a bowl, mix together cream cheese and shredded cheddar cheese.
2. Stuff each jalapeño half with the cheese mixture.
3. Wrap each stuffed jalapeño with a half-slice of bacon and secure with toothpicks.

4. Place the jalapeños in the Ninja Foodi Cooker on the sear/sauté function at medium temperature.
5. Cook for 10 minutes, turning occasionally until bacon is crispy.
6. Switch to the slow cook function and cook on low for an additional 1.5 hours.
7. Serve the cheesy bacon-wrapped jalapeños warm.

Nutritional Value (Amount per Serving):

Calories: 609; Fat: 54.48; Carb: 13.89; Protein: 21.38

Asian-Inspired Meatball Lettuce Wraps

Prep Time: 20 Minutes   Cook Time: 2 Hours   Serves: 4-6

Ingredients:

- 1.5 lbs ground chicken or turkey
- 1 cup breadcrumbs
- 2 green onions, finely chopped
- 2 tablespoons soy sauce
- 1 tablespoon hoisin sauce
- 1 tablespoon sesame oil
- 1 teaspoon ginger, grated
- 1 teaspoon garlic powder
- Iceberg lettuce leaves for wrapping

Directions:

1. In a bowl, combine ground meat, breadcrumbs, chopped green onions, soy sauce, hoisin sauce, sesame oil, grated ginger, and garlic powder.
2. Shape the mixture into meatballs and sear in the Ninja Foodi Cooker on the sear/sauté function at medium temperature until browned.
3. Transfer to the slow cook function and cook on low for 2 hours.
4. Serve the Asian-inspired meatballs in iceberg lettuce leaves.

Nutritional Value (Amount per Serving):

Calories: 465; Fat: 39.75; Carb: 12.87; Protein: 14.4

Caprese Dip

Prep Time: 15 Minutes   Cook Time: 1 Hour 30 Minutes   Serves: 6-8

Ingredients:

- 2 cups cherry tomatoes, halved
- 1 cup fresh mozzarella balls, halved
- 1/4 cup fresh basil, chopped
- 1/4 cup balsamic glaze
- Salt and pepper to taste
- Baguette slices or crackers for dipping

Directions:

1. In the Ninja Foodi Cooker on the sear/sauté function at medium temperature, combine cherry tomatoes, fresh mozzarella balls, and chopped basil.
2. Drizzle with balsamic glaze and season with salt and pepper.
3. Stir until ingredients are well coated and heated.
4. Transfer to the slow cook function and cook on low for 1.5 hours.
5. Serve the Caprese dip with baguette slices or crackers.

Nutritional Value (Amount per Serving):

Calories: 15; Fat: 0.21; Carb: 3.41; Protein: 0.46

Cajun Shrimp and Sausage Skewers

Prep Time: 20 Minutes   Cook Time: 2 Hours   Serves: 4-6

Ingredients:

- 1 lb large shrimp, peeled and deveined
- 1/2 lb smoked sausage, sliced
- 1 bell pepper, cut into chunks
- 1 red onion, cut into chunks
- Cajun seasoning to taste
- Wooden skewers, soaked in water

Directions:

1. In the Ninja Foodi Cooker on the sear/sauté function, season shrimp and sausage with Cajun seasoning.
2. Thread shrimp, sausage, bell pepper, and red onion onto wooden skewers.
3. Sear the skewers at medium temperature for 5 minutes, turning to cook evenly.
4. Transfer to the slow cook function and cook on low for 2 hours.
5. Serve the Cajun shrimp and sausage skewers hot.

Nutritional Value (Amount per Serving):

Calories: 142; Fat: 8.42; Carb: 9.67; Protein: 9.39

Sweet and Spicy Pineapple Salsa

Prep Time: 15 Minutes   Cook Time: 1 Hour 30 Minutes   Serves: 6-8

Ingredients:

- 2 cups fresh pineapple, diced
- 1 cup red bell pepper, diced
- 1/2 cup red onion, finely chopped
- 1 jalapeño, seeded and minced

- 1/4 cup fresh cilantro, chopped
- Juice of 1 lime
- 1 tablespoon honey
- Salt and pepper to taste
- Tortilla chips for serving

Directions:

1. In the Ninja Foodi Cooker on the sear/sauté function, combine pineapple, red bell pepper, red onion, jalapeño, and cilantro.
2. Sauté at medium temperature for 5 minutes until the ingredients are slightly softened.
3. Add lime juice, honey, salt, and pepper. Stir to combine.
4. Transfer to the slow cook function and cook on low for 1.5 hours.
5. Serve the sweet and spicy pineapple salsa with tortilla chips.

Nutritional Value (Amount per Serving):

Calories: 86; Fat: 1.06; Carb: 19.76; Protein: 1.08

Cajun Crab Dip

Prep Time: 20 Minutes   Cook Time: 1 Hour 30 Minutes   Serves: 6-8

Ingredients:

- 1 lb lump crab meat, drained
- 1 cup cream cheese, softened
- 1/2 cup mayonnaise
- 1/4 cup sour cream
- 1 cup shredded Monterey Jack cheese
- 2 green onions, finely chopped
- 1 tablespoon Cajun seasoning
- 1 teaspoon Worcestershire sauce
- Crackers or sliced baguette for dipping

Directions:

1. In the Ninja Foodi Cooker on the sear/sauté function at medium temperature, combine crab meat, cream cheese, mayonnaise, sour cream, shredded Monterey Jack cheese, green onions, Cajun seasoning, and Worcestershire sauce.
2. Stir until the mixture is well combined and heated through.
3. Transfer to the slow cook function and cook on low for 1.5 hours.
4. Stir occasionally and serve the Cajun crab dip with crackers or sliced baguette.

Nutritional Value (Amount per Serving):

Calories: 453; Fat: 23.98; Carb: 29.58; Protein: 33.34

Garlic Parmesan Chicken Wings

Prep Time: 15 Minutes   Cook Time: 1 Hour 30 Minutes   Serves: 4-6

Ingredients:

- 2 lbs chicken wings
- 1/2 cup grated Parmesan cheese
- 1/4 cup melted butter
- 3 cloves garlic, minced
- 1 teaspoon dried oregano
- 1 teaspoon dried parsley
- Salt and pepper to taste
- Ranch dressing for dipping

Directions:

1. In a bowl, mix together grated Parmesan cheese, melted butter, minced garlic, dried oregano, dried parsley, salt, and pepper.
2. Place chicken wings in the Ninja Foodi Cooker on the sear/sauté function at medium temperature and cook until browned.
3. Pour the Parmesan mixture over the wings and stir to coat.
4. Switch to the slow cook function and cook on low for 1.5 hours.
5. Serve the garlic Parmesan chicken wings with ranch dressing for dipping.

Nutritional Value (Amount per Serving):

Calories: 383; Fat: 20.99; Carb: 3.32; Protein: 43.2

Teriyaki Beef Skewers

Prep Time: 20 Minutes   Cook Time: 2 Hours   Serves: 4-6

Ingredients:

- 1.5 lbs beef sirloin, cut into cubes
- 1/2 cup teriyaki sauce
- 1/4 cup soy sauce
- 2 tablespoons honey
- 2 cloves garlic, minced
- 1 teaspoon ginger, grated
- Wooden skewers, soaked in water
- Sesame seeds and green onions for garnish

Directions:

1. Set the Ninja Foodi Cooker on the sear/sauté function at medium temperature.
2. In a bowl, mix teriyaki sauce, soy sauce, honey, minced garlic, and grated ginger.
3. Thread beef cubes onto wooden skewers and sear for 5 minutes, turning to brown evenly.
4. Pour the teriyaki sauce mixture over the skewers and stir to coat.

5. Switch to the slow cook function and cook on low for 2 hours.
6. Garnish with sesame seeds and chopped green onions before serving.

Nutritional Value (Amount per Serving):

Calories: 383; Fat: 20.94; Carb: 15.71; Protein: 32.03

Buffalo Cauliflower Dip

Prep Time: 15 Minutes   Cook Time: 1 Hour 30 Minutes   Serves: 6-8

Ingredients:

- 1 medium cauliflower, cut into florets
- 1 cup buffalo sauce
- 1/2 cup cream cheese, softened
- 1/2 cup shredded cheddar cheese
- 1/4 cup mayonnaise
- 1 teaspoon garlic powder
- 1 teaspoon onion powder
- Tortilla chips or celery sticks for dipping

Directions:

1. Set the Ninja Foodi Cooker on the sear/sauté function at medium temperature, mix buffalo sauce, cream cheese, shredded cheddar cheese, mayonnaise, garlic powder, and onion powder.
2. Add cauliflower florets and stir until they are well coated with the sauce.
3. Switch to the slow cook function and cook on low for 1.5 hours.
4. Stir occasionally and serve the buffalo cauliflower dip with tortilla chips or celery sticks.

Nutritional Value (Amount per Serving):

Calories: 221; Fat: 10.47; Carb: 26.76; Protein: 6.22

Loaded Potato Skins

Prep Time: 20 Minutes   Cook Time: 2 Hours   Serves: 4-6

Ingredients:

- 6 large russet potatoes, baked and halved
- 1 cup shredded cheddar cheese
- 1/2 cup sour cream
- 1/4 cup chopped green onions
- 6 slices bacon, cooked and crumbled
- Salt and pepper to taste

Directions:

1. Set the Ninja Foodi Cooker on the slow cook function.
2. Scoop out the flesh from the baked potato halves, leaving a thin layer.
3. Mix shredded cheddar cheese, sour cream, chopped green onions, and crumbled bacon.
4. Stuff each potato skin with the mixture.
5. Cook on low for 2 hours.
6. Season with salt and pepper before serving.

Nutritional Value (Amount per Serving):

Calories: 556; Fat: 18.21; Carb: 82.48; Protein: 18.46

Spinach and Feta Stuffed Peppers

Prep Time: 15 Minutes   Cook Time: 1 Hour 30 Minutes   Serves: 4-6

Ingredients:

- 6 bell peppers, halved and seeds removed
- 2 cups fresh spinach, chopped
- 1 cup feta cheese, crumbled
- 1/2 cup ricotta cheese
- 1/4 cup pine nuts, toasted
- 2 cloves garlic, minced
- 1 teaspoon dried oregano
- Olive oil for drizzling

Directions:

1. Set the Ninja Foodi Cooker on the slow cook function.
2. Combine chopped spinach, feta cheese, ricotta cheese, pine nuts, minced garlic, and dried oregano in a bowl.
3. Stuff each bell pepper half with the spinach and feta mixture.
4. Drizzle olive oil over the stuffed peppers.
5. Transfer to the cooker and cook on low for 1.5 hours.
6. Serve the spinach and feta stuffed peppers warm.

Nutritional Value (Amount per Serving):

Calories: 245; Fat: 20.07; Carb: 8.94; Protein: 9.5

Chapter 8: Desserts

Apple Cinnamon Bread Pudding

Prep Time: 15 Minutes   Cook Time: 3 Hours   Serves: 8-10

Ingredients:

- 8 cups cubed stale bread
- 3 large apples, peeled and diced
- 1 cup raisins
- 4 large eggs
- 2 cups whole milk
- 1 cup brown sugar
- 1/4 cup unsalted butter, melted
- 1 teaspoon ground cinnamon
- 1/2 teaspoon nutmeg
- 1 teaspoon vanilla extract

Directions:

1. Grease the cooker and layer cubed bread, diced apples, and raisins.
2. In a bowl, whisk together eggs, milk, brown sugar, melted butter, cinnamon, nutmeg, and vanilla extract.
3. Pour the egg mixture over the bread and apples, ensuring even coverage.
4. Cover and cook on the slow cook setting for 3 hours on low or until the pudding is set.
5. Serve warm, optionally with a scoop of vanilla ice cream.

Nutritional Value (Amount per Serving):

Calories: 321; Fat: 8.31; Carb: 57.29; Protein: 6.01

Cherry Almond Cobbler

Prep Time: 20 Minutes   Cook Time: 2 Hours 30 Minutes   Serves: 6-8

Ingredients:

- 4 cups pitted cherries, halved
- 1/2 cup granulated sugar
- 1 tablespoon cornstarch
- 1 teaspoon almond extract
- 1 cup all-purpose flour
- 1/2 cup rolled oats
- 1/2 cup sliced almonds
- 1/2 cup unsalted butter, softened

Directions:

1. Combine cherries, sugar, cornstarch, and almond extract. Place in the slow cooker.
2. In a bowl, mix flour, oats, sliced almonds, and softened butter to create the cobbler topping.
3. Spread the topping over the cherries in the slow cooker.
4. Cover and cook on the slow cook setting for 2.5 hours on low or until the cherries are tender.
5. Serve with a dollop of whipped cream.

Nutritional Value (Amount per Serving):

Calories: 245; Fat: 9.73; Carb: 38.76; Protein: 4.67

Pumpkin Spice Rice Pudding

Prep Time: 10 Minutes   Cook Time: 2 Hours 30 Minutes   Serves: 4-6

Ingredients:

- 1 cup arborio rice
- 4 cups whole milk
- 1 cup canned pumpkin puree
- 1/2 cup brown sugar
- 1 teaspoon pumpkin pie spice
- 1/4 teaspoon salt
- 1 teaspoon vanilla extract
- Whipped cream for garnish

Directions:

1. Rinse rice and place it in the cooker.
2. In a bowl, whisk together milk, pumpkin puree, brown sugar, pumpkin pie spice, salt, and vanilla extract.
3. Pour the pumpkin mixture over the rice, stirring to combine.
4. Cover and cook on the slow cook setting for 2.5 hours on low or until the rice is tender.
5. Garnish with a dollop of whipped cream before serving.

Nutritional Value (Amount per Serving):

Calories: 369; Fat: 12.36; Carb: 63.52; Protein: 9.72

Mixed Berry Cheesecake

Prep Time: 20 Minutes   Cook Time: 3 Hours   Serves: 8-10

Ingredients:

- 2 cups graham cracker crumbs
- 1/2 cup unsalted butter, melted
- 3 packages (8 oz each) cream cheese, softened
- 1 cup granulated sugar
- 3 large eggs
- 1 teaspoon vanilla extract
- 1 cup mixed berries (blueberries, strawberries, raspberries)
- 1/4 cup fruit preserves (apricot or strawberry)

Directions:

1. In a bowl, mix graham cracker crumbs with melted butter and press into the bottom of the cooker.
2. In another bowl, beat cream cheese and sugar until smooth. Add eggs one at a time, beating well after each addition. Stir in vanilla extract.
3. Pour the cream cheese mixture over the crust in the cooker.
4. In a separate bowl, toss mixed berries with fruit preserves and spoon over the cream cheese layer.

5. Cover and cook on the slow cook setting for 3 hours on low or until the cheesecake is set.
6. Allow to cool before refrigerating. Serve chilled.

Nutritional Value (Amount per Serving):

Calories: 303; Fat: 19.45; Carb: 28.83; Protein: 4.07

Chocolate Hazelnut Pudding Cake

Prep Time: 15 Minutes   Cook Time: 2 Hours 30 Minutes   Serves: 6-8

Ingredients:

- 1 cup all-purpose flour
- 1/2 cup granulated sugar
- 1/4 cup cocoa powder
- 2 teaspoons baking powder
- 1/4 teaspoon salt
- 1/2 cup milk
- 1/4 cup hazelnut spread (Nutella)
- 1/4 cup unsalted butter, melted
- 1 teaspoon vanilla extract
- 1/2 cup chopped hazelnuts
- 1 cup hot water

Directions:

1. In a mixing bowl, whisk together flour, sugar, cocoa powder, baking powder, and salt.
2. Add milk, hazelnut spread, melted butter, and vanilla extract. Mix until smooth.
3. Stir in chopped hazelnuts and spread the batter evenly in the cooker.
4. In a separate bowl, mix hot water and additional sugar. Pour over the batter in the cooker without stirring.
5. Cover and cook on the slow cook setting for 2.5 hours on low or until the cake is set.

Nutritional Value (Amount per Serving):

Calories: 280; Fat: 15.03; Carb: 33.29; Protein: 5.31

Raspberry Lemon Cheesecake Bars

Prep Time: 20 Minutes   Cook Time: 3 Hours   Serves: 8-10

Ingredients:

- 2 cups graham cracker crumbs
- 1/2 cup unsalted butter, melted
- 3 packages (8 oz each) cream cheese, softened
- 1 cup granulated sugar
- 3 large eggs

- 1 teaspoon vanilla extract
- Zest of 2 lemons
- 1 cup fresh raspberries
- Powdered sugar for dusting

Directions:

1. Mix graham cracker crumbs with melted butter and press into the bottom of the cooker.
2. In a bowl, beat cream cheese and sugar until smooth. Add eggs one at a time, beating well after each addition. Stir in vanilla extract and lemon zest.
3. Pour the cream cheese mixture over the crust in the cooker.
4. Drop raspberries evenly over the cream cheese layer.
5. Cover and cook on the slow cook setting for 3 hours on low or until the cheesecake is set.
6. Allow to cool before refrigerating. Dust with powdered sugar before serving.

Nutritional Value (Amount per Serving):

Calories: 273; Fat: 17.98; Carb: 25.29; Protein: 4.04

Pecan Pie Pudding

Prep Time: 15 Minutes   Cook Time: 2 Hours 30 Minutes   Serves: 6-8

Ingredients:

- 1 cup chopped pecans
- 1 cup light corn syrup
- 1/2 cup packed brown sugar
- 1/4 cup unsalted butter, melted
- 3 large eggs
- 1 teaspoon vanilla extract
- 1/4 teaspoon salt
- 1 cup heavy cream

Directions:

1. Sprinkle chopped pecans in the bottom of the cooker.
2. In a bowl, whisk together corn syrup, brown sugar, melted butter, eggs, vanilla extract, and salt.
3. Pour the mixture over the pecans in the cooker.
4. Pour heavy cream over the top.
5. Cover and cook on the slow cook setting for 2.5 hours on low or until the pudding is set.
6. Serve warm, optionally with a scoop of vanilla ice cream.

Nutritional Value (Amount per Serving):

Calories: 420; Fat: 22.96; Carb: 55.6; Protein: 3.09

Banana Foster Bread Pudding

Prep Time: 15 Minutes   Cook Time: 3 Hours   Serves: 8-10

Ingredients:

- 8 cups cubed French bread
- 4 ripe bananas, sliced
- 1 cup chopped pecans
- 4 large eggs
- 2 cups whole milk
- 1 cup granulated sugar
- 1/4 cup unsalted butter, melted
- 1 teaspoon vanilla extract
- 1/4 cup dark rum (optional)

Directions:

1. Grease the cooker and layer cubed bread, sliced bananas, and chopped pecans.
2. In a bowl, whisk together eggs, milk, sugar, melted butter, vanilla extract, and rum (if using).
3. Pour the egg mixture over the bread and bananas, ensuring even coverage.
4. Cover and cook on the slow cook setting for 3 hours on low or until the pudding is set.
5. Serve warm, optionally drizzled with caramel sauce.

Nutritional Value (Amount per Serving):

Calories: 477; Fat: 19.2; Carb: 63.64; Protein: 11.53

Coconut Rice Pudding with Mango

Prep Time: 10 Minutes   Cook Time: 2 Hours 30 Minutes   Serves: 4-6

Ingredients:

- 1 cup jasmine rice
- 4 cups coconut milk
- 1/2 cup granulated sugar
- 1/2 cup shredded coconut
- 1 teaspoon vanilla extract
- 1/4 teaspoon salt
- 1 ripe mango, peeled and diced
- Fresh mint leaves for garnish

Directions:

1. Rinse rice and place it in the cooker.
2. In a saucepan, heat coconut milk, sugar, shredded coconut, vanilla extract, and salt until it simmers. Pour over the rice.
3. Stir well and cover. Cook on the slow cook setting for 2.5 hours on low or until the rice is tender.
4. Before serving, top with diced mango and garnish with fresh mint leaves.

Nutritional Value (Amount per Serving):

Calories: 582; Fat: 50.88; Carb: 38.36; Protein: 8.09

Triple Chocolate Brownie Pudding

Prep Time: 15 Minutes   Cook Time: 2 Hours 30 Minutes   Serves: 6-8

Ingredients:

- 11 cup all-purpose flour
- 1/2 cup cocoa powder
- 1 cup granulated sugar
- 1/2 teaspoon baking powder
- 1/4 teaspoon salt
- 1/2 cup unsalted butter, melted
- 2 large eggs
- 1 teaspoon vanilla extract
- 1/2 cup milk chocolate chips
- 1/2 cup dark chocolate chips
- 1/2 cup white chocolate chips

Directions:

1. In a mixing bowl, whisk together flour, cocoa powder, sugar, baking powder, and salt.
2. Add melted butter, eggs, and vanilla extract. Mix until well combined.
3. Stir in milk chocolate chips, dark chocolate chips, and white chocolate chips.
4. Spread the batter evenly in the cooker.
5. Cover and cook on the slow cook setting for 2.5 hours on low or until the brownie is set.

Nutritional Value (Amount per Serving):

Calories: 1023; Fat: 20.26; Carb: 185.37; Protein: 24.52

Salted Caramel Apple

Prep Time: 20 Minutes   Cook Time: 3 Hours   Serves: 6-8

Ingredients:

- 6 cups peeled and sliced apples
- 1/2 cup granulated sugar
- 1/4 cup all-purpose flour
- 1 teaspoon ground cinnamon
- 1/2 cup caramel sauce (store-bought or homemade)
- 1 cup old-fashioned oats
- 1/2 cup all-purpose flour
- 1/2 cup packed brown sugar
- 1/2 cup unsalted butter, melted
- 1/2 teaspoon sea salt

Directions:

1. Toss sliced apples with granulated sugar, flour, and cinnamon. Place in the cooker.

2. Drizzle caramel sauce over the apples.
3. In a bowl, combine oats, flour, brown sugar, melted butter, and sea salt to make the crisp topping.
4. Sprinkle the topping over the apples in the cooker.
5. Cover and cook on the slow cook setting for 3 hours on low or until the apples are tender.
6. Serve warm with a scoop of vanilla ice cream.

Nutritional Value (Amount per Serving):

Calories: 304; Fat: 10.09; Carb: 56.11; Protein: 4.8

Espresso Chocolate Mousse

Prep Time: 15 Minutes   Cook Time: 2 Hours   Serves: 4-6

Ingredients:

- 1 cup dark chocolate chips
- 1/4 cup strong brewed espresso
- 3 large eggs, separated
- 1/4 cup granulated sugar
- 1 teaspoon vanilla extract
- Pinch of salt
- Whipped cream and chocolate shavings for garnish

Directions:

1. Melt dark chocolate chips with brewed espresso in a heatproof bowl. Allow to cool slightly.
2. In another bowl, beat egg yolks, sugar, vanilla extract, and a pinch of salt until light and fluffy.
3. Gradually add the melted chocolate mixture to the egg yolk mixture, mixing well.
4. In a separate bowl, beat egg whites until stiff peaks form. Gently fold into the chocolate mixture.
5. Pour the mousse into individual serving glasses.
6. Cover and cook on the slow cook setting for 2 hours on low or until the mousse is set.
7. Chill in the refrigerator before serving. Garnish with whipped cream and chocolate shavings.

Nutritional Value (Amount per Serving):

Calories: 247; Fat: 13.35; Carb: 28.14; Protein: 3.28

Peach Cobbler with Almond Streusel

Prep Time: 20 Minutes   Cook Time: 2 Hours 30 Minutes   Serves: 6-8

Ingredients:

- 4 cups peeled and sliced peaches
- 1/2 cup granulated sugar
- 1 tablespoon cornstarch
- 1 teaspoon almond extract
- 1 cup all-purpose flour
- 1/2 cup rolled oats
- 1/2 cup sliced almonds
- 1/2 cup unsalted butter, softened

Directions:

1. Toss sliced peaches with sugar, cornstarch, and almond extract. Place in the cooker.
2. In a bowl, mix flour, oats, sliced almonds, and softened butter to create the streusel topping.
3. Spread the streusel over the peaches in the cooker.
4. Cover and cook on the slow cook setting for 2.5 hours on low or until the peaches are tender.
5. Serve with a scoop of vanilla ice cream.

Nutritional Value (Amount per Serving):

Calories: 306; Fat: 9.74; Carb: 56.15; Protein: 4.27

Lemon Blueberry Cheesecake

Prep Time: 20 Minutes   Cook Time: 3 Hours   Serves: 8-10

Ingredients:

- 2 cups graham cracker crumbs
- 1/2 cup unsalted butter, melted
- 3 packages (8 oz each) cream cheese, softened
- 1 cup granulated sugar
- 3 large eggs
- 1 teaspoon vanilla extract
- Zest of 1 lemon
- 1 cup fresh blueberries
- Lemon curd for topping

Directions:

1. Mix graham cracker crumbs with melted butter and press into the bottom of the cooker.
2. In a bowl, beat cream cheese and sugar until smooth. Add eggs one at a time, beating well after each addition. Stir in vanilla extract and lemon zest.

3. Pour the cream cheese mixture over the crust in the cooker.
4. Scatter fresh blueberries over the cream cheese layer.
5. Cover and cook on the slow cook setting for 3 hours on low or until the cheesecake is set.
6. Allow to cool before refrigerating. Top with a layer of lemon curd before serving.

Nutritional Value (Amount per Serving):

Calories: 241; Fat: 16.04; Carb: 21.83; Protein: 3.54

Coconut Tapioca Pudding

Prep Time: 20 Minutes   Cook Time: 2 Hours 30 Minutes   Serves: 4-6

Ingredients:

- 1/2 cup small pearl tapioca
- 2 cans (28 oz each) coconut milk
- 1/2 cup granulated sugar
- 1/4 teaspoon salt
- 1 teaspoon vanilla extract
- Toasted coconut flakes for garnish

Directions:

1. Rinse tapioca and place it in the cooker.
2. In a saucepan, combine coconut milk, sugar, salt, and vanilla extract. Heat until it simmers. Pour over the tapioca.
3. Stir well and cover. Cook on the slow cook setting for 2.5 hours on low or until the tapioca is translucent.
4. Serve warm or chilled, garnished with toasted coconut flakes.

Nutritional Value (Amount per Serving):

Calories: 487; Fat: 39,44; Carb: 35.3; Protein: 3.84

Mint Chocolate Chip Pudding Cake

Prep Time: 15 Minutes   Cook Time: 2 Hours 30 Minutes   Serves: 6-8

Ingredients:

- 1 cup all-purpose flour
- 1/2 cup cocoa powder
- 1 cup granulated sugar
- 1/2 teaspoon baking powder
- 1/4 teaspoon salt
- 1/2 cup unsalted butter, melted
- 2 large eggs
- 1 teaspoon peppermint extract
- 1/2 cup milk chocolate chips
- 1/2 cup mint chocolate chips
- 1 cup hot water

Directions:

1. In a mixing bowl, whisk together flour, cocoa powder, sugar, baking

powder, and salt.

2. Add melted butter, eggs, and peppermint extract. Mix until well combined.
3. Stir in milk chocolate chips and mint chocolate chips.
4. Spread the batter evenly in the cooker.
5. In a separate bowl, mix hot water and additional sugar. Pour over the batter in the slow cooker without stirring.
6. Cover and cook on the slow cook setting for 2.5 hours on low or until the cake is set.

Nutritional Value (Amount per Serving):

Calories: 252; Fat: 11.61; Carb: 35.44; Protein: 5.06

Orange Cranberry Bread Pudding

Prep Time: 20 Minutes   Cook Time: 3 Hours   Serves: 8-10

Ingredients:

- 8 cups cubed stale bread
- 1 cup dried cranberries
- Zest of 2 oranges
- 4 large eggs
- 2 cups whole milk
- 1 cup granulated sugar
- 1/4 cup unsalted butter, melted
- 1 teaspoon vanilla extract
- Orange glaze (powdered sugar mixed with orange juice)

Directions:

1. Grease the cooker and layer cubed bread, dried cranberries, and orange zest.
2. In a bowl, whisk together eggs, milk, sugar, melted butter, and vanilla extract.
3. Pour the egg mixture over the bread and cranberries, ensuring even coverage.
4. Cover and cook on the slow cook setting for 3 hours on low or until the pudding is set.
5. Drizzle with orange glaze before serving.

Nutritional Value (Amount per Serving):

Calories: 287; Fat: 8.26; Carb: 47.17; Protein: 6.33

Almond Joy Rice Pudding

Prep Time: 15 Minutes   Cook Time: 2 Hours 30 Minutes   Serves: 4-6

- 1 cup Arborio rice
- 4 cups coconut milk
- 1/2 cup granulated sugar
- 1/2 cup shredded coconut
- 1/2 cup chopped almonds
- 1 teaspoon almond extract
- 1/4 teaspoon salt
- Chocolate sauce for drizzling

Directions:

1. Rinse rice and place it in the cooker.
2. In a saucepan, heat coconut milk, sugar, shredded coconut, chopped almonds, almond extract, and salt until it braises. Pour over the rice.
3. Stir well and cover. Cook on the slow cook setting for 2.5 hours on low or until the rice is tender.
4. Serve warm, drizzled with chocolate sauce.

Nutritional Value (Amount per Serving):

Calories: 578; Fat: 50.99; Carb: 37.01; Protein: 7.92

Pumpkin Caramel Bread Pudding

Prep Time: 20 Minutes   Cook Time: 3 Hours   Serves: 8-10

Ingredients:

- 8 cups cubed stale bread
- 1 cup canned pumpkin puree
- 1 cup brown sugar
- 4 large eggs
- 2 cups whole milk
- 1/4 cup unsalted butter, melted
- 1 teaspoon pumpkin pie spice
- 1/4 teaspoon salt
- Caramel sauce for drizzling

Directions:

1. Grease the cooker and layer cubed bread.
2. In a bowl, mix pumpkin puree, brown sugar, eggs, milk, melted butter, pumpkin pie spice, and salt.
3. Pour the pumpkin mixture over the bread, ensuring even coverage.
4. Cover and cook on the slow cook setting for 3 hours on low or until the pudding is set.
5. Drizzle with caramel sauce before serving.

Nutritional Value (Amount per Serving):

Calories: 291; Fat: 8.24; Carb: 49.17; Protein: 6.16

White Chocolate Raspberry Cheesecake

Prep Time: 20 Minutes   Cook Time: 3 Hours   Serves: 8-10

Ingredients:

- 2 cups graham cracker crumbs
- 1/2 cup unsalted butter, melted
- 3 packages (8 oz each) cream cheese, softened
- 1 cup granulated sugar
- 3 large eggs
- 1 teaspoon vanilla extract
- 1 cup white chocolate chips, melted
- 1 cup fresh raspberries
- White chocolate ganache for topping

Directions:

1. Mix graham cracker crumbs with melted butter and press into the bottom of the cooker.
2. In a bowl, beat cream cheese and sugar until smooth. Add eggs one at a time, beating well after each addition. Stir in vanilla extract.
3. Pour the cream cheese mixture over the crust in the cooker.
4. Drizzle melted white chocolate over the cream cheese layer.
5. Scatter fresh raspberries over the top.
6. Cover and cook on the slow cook setting for 3 hours on low or until the cheesecake is set.
7. Allow to cool before refrigerating. Drizzle with white chocolate ganache before serving.

Nutritional Value (Amount per Serving):

Calories: 385; Fat: 23.03; Carb: 34.52; Protein: 4.85

APPENDIX RECIPE INDEX

Made in the USA
Monee, IL
11 November 2024

69867639R00061